THE LAST STEAM
LOCOMOTIVES OF
BRITISH RAILWAYS

B.R. 2-10-0 No. 92220 EVENING STAR Class 9F.

This was the last steam locomotive built for British Railways. It was completed at Swindon Works, formerly of the Great Western Railway and below each of the nameplates on the smoke deflectors were plaques which read:—

No. 92220 BUILT AT SWINDON
MARCH 1960

THE LAST STEAM LOCOMOTIVE FOR
BRITISH RAILWAYS

NAMED AT SWINDON ON MARCH 18th
1960 BY K. W. C. GRAND, ESQ,

MEMBER OF THE BRITISH TRANSPORT
COMMISSION

THE LAST STEAM LOCOMOTIVES OF BRITISH RAILWAYS

P. RANSOME-WALLIS

LONDON

IAN ALLAN LTD

First published 1966
Fourth impression 1988

ISBN 0 7110 0475 7

Published by Ian Allan Ltd, Shepperton, Surrey; and
printed by Ian Allan Printing Ltd at their works at
Coombelands in Runnymede, England

Dedicated to the Memory of British Steam Locomotives
which gave so much pleasure to so many.

CONTENTS

All the Photographs are by the Author unless otherwise acknowledged.

PREFACE

The ideas behind this book are:

1. To illustrate examples of locomotive classes which became the last steam locomotives of British Railways. No attempt has been made to illustrate examples of every class and its modifications. The purpose has been to show a good selection of what was working during the period under review.

2. To provide some pertinent information about each class illustrated and, at the beginning of each section, to provide some background information about each type.

3. To give more detailed information about the more important classes and to provide illustrations of their history in some instances. Where such photographs show locomotives which had ceased to exist in that form before 1955 the plate number is given a suffix e.g. 12A shows a Southern Class T9 before reconstruction.

4. To show the last steam locomotives in as many different styles of painting, numbering and lettering as possible. This is an aspect of locomotive study which to me has no interest, but as I know there are many to whom these matters greatly appeal, I hope my selection will please them. No liveries are shown which go back before 1923 except in the case of two preserved locomotives which were in revenue-earning service after 1955.

The date at which the book begins is 1955–56. In 1955 the British Railways Modernisation Plan was published and no new designs for steam power were made after that time. Existing building programmes were, in the main, completed and the last steam locomotive was turned into traffic on March 19th, 1960.

No attempt has been made to give lists of numbers, dates of scrapping or final allocations. This aspect of the art has received its very full share of documentation in the many excellent journals of the railway societies and elsewhere.

The plan of the book is to show locomotives by types beginning with 2—4—0, then 4—4—0, 4—4—2, 0—6—0, 2—6—0 and so on, considering tender engines and tank engines as two separate groups. The types are graded by their British Railways power groups starting with the lowest numbers and working upwards.

During the last few years I have frequently been asked to repeat one of my earliest books *Locomotives Through the Lens*, long since out of print. It was, I think, a poor effort but some of its content was worthy of better treatment and presentation. As this book, in some ways, follows the plan of that earlier work, I have included a few of the photographs which appeared in it.

Compiling a book of this sort inevitably brings back many memories—most of them happy—of the miles travelled on the footplate, of the excitement of a Shed or a Works visit to see a new engine, of the many happy hours spent by the side of the line on sunny afternoons. I hope, very sincerely, that it will bring similar memories to those who read it.

Herne Bay
1966.

P. R-W.

2. **L.N.E.** B.R. No. 62790 Class E4 on a Mark's Tey to Sudbury train near Wakes Colne.

The 2—4—0 type was widely used in Britain for mixed traffic and express passenger duties in the latter part of the nineteenth and the first two decades of the twentieth centuries.

Famous among such locomotives were the Kirtley and Johnson 2—4—0s of the Midland Railway, many of which came into the L.M.S.R. and three of the Johnson engines were taken into British Railways stock in 1948.

Most famous of all 2—4—0s were the engines of the London and North Western Railway officially known as the *Precedent* Class but frequently referred to as the " Jumbos ". They had 6ft 6in driving wheels, were capable of high speeds and of hauling enormous loads relative to their size. They were, not surprisingly, very heavy on coal but even in L.M.S. days *Precedents* were to be seen, acting as pilots to various modern locomotives on important duties. They were all taken out of service long before nationalisation.

The Southern had no 2—4—0s but the London, Brighton and South Coast and the London and South Western Railways contributed a few 0—4—2s which may perhaps be regarded as a " variation on a theme ".

The Great Western 2—4—0s which came into the Grouping period were mostly of Dean's *Barnum* Class with sandwich frames and introduced in 1889. All of them were scrapped before the Second War began. Great Western 2—4—0s which did, however, come into British Railways stock were three elegant little machines which had been absorbed by the G.W. from the Midland and South Western Junction Railway. Adorned with G.W. fittings they worked the Lambourn Branch for many years, but all were withdrawn before 1955.

So to the London and North Eastern Railway and the only 2—4—0s which survived to be among the last steam locomotives of British Railways. These were Class T26 of the former Great Eastern Railway and eighteen came into British Railways stock in 1948 as Class E4; ten were in service in 1955 mostly working on the branch lines of Cambridgeshire and the Eastern Counties. They were designed by J. Holden as a mixed traffic version (5ft 8in wheels) of his 7ft 2—4—0 express engines of Class T19. One hundred were built between 1891 and 1902. As built they had stove-pipe chimneys and the only major visible alterations during their long lives were the provision of lipped chimneys, pop safety valves, and of side window cabs to those engines which in L.N.E.R. days, were sent to work over the Pennines between Darlington and Tebay.

4—4—0

The first 4—4—0 in Britain was built for the Ottoman Railway from Smyrna to Aidin by Robert Stephenson in 1859. Ten were ordered, but the Ottoman Railway could only afford to purchase six and the London Chatham and Dover Railway bought the remaining four. The first one in service was named AEOLUS and before it was sold to the L.C. and D. it ran trials in the North East and was seen by the engineers of several Companies. As a result Stephensons built similar engines for the Stockton and Darlington Railway and for the Great North of Scotland Railway during the next two years.

Many of the early engines had outside cylinders, but over the years the pattern changed completely and the great majority of 2-cylinder 4—4—0s remaining in the twentieth century on British railways, had inside cylinders. Notable exceptions were Adams' beautiful London and South Western engines of 1880 and later, Beyer Peacock's little " A " Class engines for the Midland and Great Northern, first built in 1881 and a few of the Great North of Scotland engines of 1866. Only one modern outside cylinder class was built—G. J. Churchward's *County* Class for the Great Western which went into service between 1904 and 1912.

Despite the overwhelming preponderence of the 2-cylinder simple 4—4—0s in recent times, almost every other arrangement of cylinders has been tried; 3-cylinder simples e.g. the Southern *Schools* Class, will be referred to later; 4-cylinder simples were comparatively rare, the Glasgow and South Western had one which lasted well into modern times, albeit in a rebuilt form and the London and South Western had some 4-cylinder engines with uncoupled driving wheels which were more accurately, 4—2—2—0 than 4—4—0.

Compounds have been of the 2-cylinder (e.g. on the North Eastern), 3-cylinder (e.g. Midland and also North Eastern), and 4-cylinder (e.g. London and North Western) varieties and the high pressure cylinders have been inside the frames as in Midland practice and outside as on the North Western. The North British Railway could boast of having the only 4-cylinder tandem compound 4—4—0 ever to run in Britain (although the Great Western had two 2—4—0s). It was converted from a simple engine by Holmes in 1885 and the four cylinders were placed between the frames so it was difficult to distinguish it from an ordinary 2-cylinder simple.

The reasons for most 4—4—0s having the cylinders between the frames were probably mainly twofold. First, British designers had almost a mania for building beautiful machines with elegant lines and with as much of the " works " as possible tucked away out of sight, regardless of the maintenance and repair problems created by such a policy. Second, with plate frames and often the need to keep axle loading to a minimum, it was certainly advantageous mechanically to keep the piston thrust as near to the centre line of the locomotive as possible, despite the cost and disadvantages of having to make a cranked axle. No doubt those who had to work on the Great Western *County's* often wished that they too had had inside cylinders as few locomotives have ever had such a wicked tendency to roll.

This inside cylinder policy ran counter to contemporary locomotive practice in the rest of the world where outside cylinders were the general rule and few railways, outside the British sphere of influence, had inside cylinder 4—4—0s. Holland might be quoted as one of the exceptions.

The development of the modern multi-cylinder 4—4—0 was unique in Britain and produced some outstanding locomotives. Of the older generation, brought up-to-date, the Johnson/Deeley/Fowler 3-cylinder compounds of the Midland and London Midland and Scottish Railways lasted well into the last days of steam and were capable of outstanding performances. R. E. L. Maunsell's 3-cylinder V Class (the *Schools*) of 1930 were, without doubt, the world's most advanced 4—4—0 design, and were able, when skillfuly driven, to surpass the performances of many larger locomotive types. Another 3-cylinder design was H. N. Gresley's 1927 *Shire* Class for the London and North Eastern Railway, many of which were later built with rotary cam poppet valves (*Hunt* Class). They also were fine engines, but never put up the performances to equal the day to day running of the Southern engines. It was interesting that, when Edward Thompson rebuilt one of the *Hunts* in 1942 with two cylinders, he put them between the frames, thus conforming to conventional British practice.

The 4—4—0 lasted longer on main line service in Britain than anywhere else in the world. The great majority of British 4—4—0s gave long and trouble-free service to the railways until they finally disappeared from normal service in 1962. Three were preserved in working order and appeared on occasion and there are several in museums, the last survivors of that peculiarly British institution—the inside cylinder 4—4—0.

3. Great Western. Double-framed 4—4—0 No. 3440 CITY OF TRURO. Built in 1903 to the design of William Dean at Swindon Works.

With H. N. Gresley's Class A4 Pacific MALLARD (**Plate 152**) No. 3440, will for always be famous as a holder of the world speed record for steam locomotives. Just for how long after her record-breaking 102·3 m.p.h. sprint down Wellington Bank on May 9th, 1904, CITY OF TRURO held the record is not certain. Long before Gresley's Pacifics started topping the hundred m.p.h. in the 1930s, the Pennsylvania R.R. and one or two other American railroads had produced authenticated logs with speeds well over the 100 mark.

It is popular now to doubt if the speed claimed for CITY OF TRURO was, in fact, attained. The records have been carefully studied by experts in train timing and it is generally agreed that, anyway, the engine exceeded "the hundred", and unlike several other locomotives which have done so, arrived mechanically sound and with cool bearings, at her destination.

CITY OF TRURO was renumbered 3717 in 1912 and a year before that she had been rebuilt with a superheater boiler and had new cylinders with piston valves in 1915. She was withdrawn in 1931, her original number was restored and she was sent to the Railway Museum at York where she remained until 1957. During that year she was taken away from York and at Swindon was overhauled and put into sound working order. For the next four years No. 3440 was used on special trains, but in between times was used in normal revenue earning service working from Didcot shed. Thus she became one of the Last Steam Locomotives of British Railways and qualifies for inclusion in this book.

In 1961, CITY OF TRURO was again withdrawn, on this occasion one suspects for all time. She has found her last resting place in the beautiful Great Western Museum at Swindon, hard by the factory which made her.

4. Great Western. In 1895 William Dean designed the *Duke* Class double-framed 4—4—0s with 5ft 7½in driving wheels for service in Devon and Cornwall. They had parallel domed boilers. Four years later appeared the first of a similar class but with coned domeless boilers, known as the *Bulldog* Class. As engines of both these classes were withdrawn, the frames of some of the *Bulldogs* were used, with new superheated domed boilers and with some parts of the *Dukes* to produce a new class of 4—4—0. After a prototype reconstruction in 1929, twenty-nine further locomotives appeared between 1936–39, and were named after noble earls.

No. 3212 EARL OF ELDON is shown when new. Later the names were removed from these engines which for many years were known as *Dukedogs* and spent most of their lives on the Cambrian lines in Wales.

5. L.N.E. The inside-cylinder 4—4—0s of Class D40 originated on the Great North of Scotland Railway. The Class consisted of two distinct batches—G.N.S. Class V introduced in 1899 by W. Pickersgill and built with saturated boilers and Class F introduced in 1920 by T. E. Heywood. Some engines of Class V were later superheated, but Class F were built with superheated boilers and piston valves. The locomotive illustrated was B.R. No. 62277 but has been restored to its G.N.S. colours and number, 49, for preservation. It is named GORDON HIGHLANDER and was one of ten D40's which remained in B.R. stock in 1955.

6. L.N.E. Probably the most handsome British 4—4—0s were the elegant Great Central locomotives designed by J. G. Robinson. The original engines were Class 11E of 1913 and known, from their names, as the *Director* Class (L.N.E. Class D10). A later series with deeper frames, double-windowed cabs and with boiler centre-line pitched $1\frac{1}{2}$in higher, was built in 1920–22 and became known as the *Improved Directors* (G.C. Class 11F, L.N.E. Class D11/1). All eleven of these later engines were at work in 1955 and the photograph shows B.R. No. 62662 PRINCE OF WALES.

7. L.N.E. After the 1923 Amalgamation, H. N. Gresley perpetuated the *Improved Directors* by ordering twenty-four locomotives from Kitson and Armstrong-Whitworth for service in Scotland. They were delivered in 1924 and the photograph shows No. 6394 (Class D11/2) as she first appeared. The chimney and boiler mountings were reduced to conform with the Scottish loading gauge. The deep coupled-wheel vallances were soon cut away on these and on all the engines of Classes D10 and D11/1. The *Scottish Directors* were given names taken from the Scott novels. All were at work in 1955, some with long travel piston valves.

8. L.N.E. In 1900, J. Holden introduced the first of the famous *Claud Hamilton* Class of 4—4—0s for the Great Eastern Railway. Officially Class S46 (L.N.E. Class D14) they had 4ft 9in diameter saturated round-top boilers. Class D56 (L.N.E. Class D15) with Belpaire boilers soon followed and were built until 1911 under the direction of S. D. Holden. Considerable rebuilding and superheating occurred over the years and in 1923 appeared A. J. Hill's version of the design, Class H88 (the *Super Clauds*), with a 5ft 1in superheater Belpaire boiler. This Class was L.N.E. D16 and from 1933, H. N. Gresley developed Class D16/3 by rebuilding engines, first of the earlier series and then the *Super Clauds* with round-top boilers and, where necessary, piston valves. Some engines had long lap valves fitted later. It was as D16/3 that these locomotives were among the "Last Steam Locomotives", though there were considerable detail variations in the class. No. 62585 is shown, working a slow train from Bletchley to Cambridge.

8A shows L.N.E. Class D15 as built with saturated Belpaire boiler. ▶

9. L.N.E. B.R. No. 62397, North Eastern Railway Class R (L.N.E. Class D20) designed by W. Worsdell and introduced, non-superheater, in 1899. Later engines were built with superheaters and the earlier ones soon received them. The R's were the most successful and economical of all North Eastern express locomotives and many drivers preferred them to the later and more powerful Atlantics and certainly to the larger 4—4—0s of Class R1. The engine shown has a tender rebuilt with tank and bunker of L.N.E. design. ▼

10. L.N.E. Class D30 North British superheated *Scott* Class B.R. No. 62426 CUDDIE HEADRIGG leaving Edinburgh (Princes Street) with a slow train for Stirling. Named after characters in the novels of Sir Walter Scott, the first *Scotts* appeared in 1909 with 190 p.s.i. saturated boilers and 19in diameter cylinders. They were designed by W. P. Reid who, in 1912, introduced a much improved version with superheaters and piston valves but with 20 p.s.i. less working pressure though the cylinders were 20in diameter. The earlier engines became L.N.E. Class D29 and all were ultimately superheated. None, however, survived until 1955, though twenty-four of the later engines (Class D30) were at work at that time. They were fine strong engines and retained their North British appearance to the end, the only major visible alteration being the removal of the smokebox wing plates.

11. L.N.E. Class D34 North British *Glen* Class B.R. No. 62474 GLEN CROE. W. P. Reid's mixed traffic version of the superheated *Scott*. They were at their best when working on the West Highland line. Twenty-seven were at work in 1955 and one is preserved.

12. Southern. Dugald Drummond was one of the world's outstanding locomotive engineers. He was locomotive Superintendent of the North British Railway from 1875 to 1882 and of the Caledonian Railway from 1882 to 1890. Many of the locomotives he designed for those companies came into British Railways stock. After four years in Australia, Drummond came home to the appointment of Chief Mechanical Engineer of the London and South Western Railway. Among the most successful of his designs for that company were the 4—4—0s of Class T9 built between 1899 and 1901. Some of these engines had firebox water tubes and there were differences between batches in splashers and sand boxes. All had the large, rather ugly, eight-wheeled tenders; the L.S.W. never had water troughs. The T9's were well-liked, free-running engines and became known as "The Greyhounds". From 1922 the locomotives were very successfully rebuilt to the design of R. W. Urie with superheater boilers and the working pressure was increased from 170 p.s.i. to 175 p.s.i. The cylinder diameter was also increased from $18\frac{1}{2}$in to 19in though the slide valves were retained.

Shown is B.R. No. 30119 which for some years was the Royal Engine.

12A shows No. 723 in much its original condition.

13. Southern. H. S. Wainwright was in charge of locomotive design on the South Eastern and Chatham Railway from 1899 until 1913. His locomotives were among the most elegant in the country, beautifully finished and with burnished brass dome covers. They were strongly built and had power reversers, but as non-superheater slide valve engines they were heavy on coal when worked at all hard. Heading a train of vintage "bird-cage" stock at Tunbridge Wells, No. 31734 still shows the characteristic grace of a bygone age even while wearing British Railways livery. She was one of Wainwright's D Class with round-top boilers and plain coupling-rods.

13A. In 1905 Wainwright introduced his E Class 4—4—0 with Belpaire boiler, extended smokebox and fluted coupling rods. They lacked some of the elegance of the earlier D Class but were more powerful engines in view of their having a slightly higher working pressure (180 p.s.i. as against 175 p.s.i.) and a slightly smaller coupled wheel diameter (6ft 6in as against 6ft 8in). Two were later superheated and given larger (20½in) cylinders. None of them survived to be among the last British steam locomotives.

14. Southern. After the First War, the South Eastern and Chatham Railway was very short of both money and suitable locomotives to work its increasingly heavy boat expresses from Victoria. Furthermore the maximum axle load allowed by the Civil Engineer over the Chatham route was 17½ tons—or that of the E Class 4—4—0 (**Plate 13A**). R. E. L. Maunsell, the Swindon-trained C.M.E. solved the problem by rebuilding one of the E Class, No. 179 with a superheater Belpaire boiler in which the original barrel was utilised but a larger firebox provided. New cylinders with 10in diameter piston valves were also provided and the weight of the rebuild, known as Class E1, was a mere 5 cwt more than that of the original engine. A further ten Class E were similarly rebuilt by Messrs. Beyer Peacock, and the Class was outstandingly successful.

The picture shows B.R. No. 31019 at work on the Kent Coast. The similar appearance of these locomotives to the Midland Class 2 (**Plate 16**) will be noted. In design of the front-end, however, there was no similarity and the Midland engines could never have achieved the performances regularly given by the South Eastern machines.

15. In 1921–22, twenty-one locomotives of Class D (**Plate 13**) were similarly rebuilt to become Class D1. The boilers were, in this case, provided with top feed and smokebox regulators but as they were interchangeable with those of the E1's the latter could often be seen with top feed boilers. The plain coupling rods of the D1's, however, made locomotives of this class readily distinguishable from the E1's with their fluted rods. Both classes originally had snifting valves on the smokebox but these were later removed. Not surprisingly, in view of the heavy work they were called upon to do, most of the rebuilds required new and stronger frames fairly early on.

B.R. No. 31727 is seen here with empty stock at Tonbridge.

16. L.M.S. The Midland Railway was one of the largest and most important of British railway systems and its locomotive policy was characterised by first, its reluctance ever to build large locomotives—it never owned an express locomotive with more than four coupled wheels—nor, with one solitary exception, a freight locomotive with more than six coupled wheels. Second, its apparent reluctance to build new locomotives. No company has ever approached the Midland in its numbers of rebuilt locomotives, but then the terms "rebuild", "reconstruction" and "replacement" are so loosely used in railway parlance that it is often difficult even to try to sort out what is really new or what may honestly be termed rebuilt. The classic case is that of the Midland 4—4—0s. From 1876 S. W. Johnson introduced many such locomotives with driving wheels 6ft 6in to 7ft 0in in diameter and with variations in boiler and cylinder dimensions. During the lives of most of these locomotives they were rebuilt at least once and often two or three times. A typical Johnson 4—4—0 originally built in 1877, and having 7ft 0in diameter driving wheels is shown in **Plate 16A** as it appeared in 1925. From 1912–23, were built the Midland Superheater Class 2 4—4—0s to the design of Henry Fowler. Officially these were described as rebuilds of various Johnson engines but as boilers, frames, cylinders and most details were obviously new, it is more correct to describe them as replacements. They had short travel piston valves, and made a most powerful and impressive noise. They ran well with light passenger trains and were extensively used for double heading. Their maintenance was very cheap probably because it was almost impossible to work them very hard.
Shown here (**Plate 16**) is B.R. No. 40562 with a Stanier chimney.

17. (Opposite, top). What were definitely new engines were the 136 Class 2 4—4—0s built for the L.M.S. to the order of Henry Fowler. Apart from some slight modification to valves and valve gear, and the reduction of driving wheel diameter from 7ft 0in to 6ft 9in, they were identical with the Midland series.

The photograph shows No. 40655 in the frequent role of pilot engine on a main line express. The train engine in this instance was No. 46161 KINGS OWN and the train an up Glasgow express near Bletchley.

18. L.M.S. J. F. McIntosh designed four famous classes of 4—4—0s for the Caledonian Railway. The first of these appeared in 1896 and was named DUNALASTAIR from the estate of that name owned by the Company Chairman. The design was developed and the next and rather larger, engines were known as the *Dunalastair II* Class, the first of the class actually carrying that name. Further development resulted in classes which became known as *Dunalastair III* and *Dunalastair IV* though no engines ever carried those names. Superheaters were applied to some engines of the *Dunalastair II, III* and *IV* Classes giving further variants. In 1910 came the 139, or *Dunalastair IV Superheater* Class of which B.R. No. 54445 is an example. They were fine engines and when built, had large double-bogie tenders which gave them an excellent and massive appearance. After McIntosh retired, William Pickersgill perpetuated the design with detail differences—straight coupling-rod splashers and in some engines, snifting valves placed behind the chimney. Examples of both McIntosh and Pickersgill engines remained in service in the last days of steam.

19. Southern. R. E. L. Maunsell's first duty on becoming C.M.E. of the South Eastern and Chatham in 1913 was to provide adequate power for the increasingly heavy boat expresses and for the Folkestone and Hastings business trains from Charing Cross. Owing to severe weight restrictions the engine had to be a 4—4—0 and a design prepared by Wainwright was slightly modified and put out to contract. Beyer Peacock built twelve and A. Borsig of Berlin, ten, which arrived in Britain partially dismantled just before the outbreak of the First War. Borsig's fitters supervised their erection at Ashford. These engines, the L Class, gave good service for many years, though until the Southern Railway strengthened bridges after 1923, the L's were too heavy to work into and out of, Victoria.
B.R. No. 31780, one of the Borsig engines is shown with an up slow train near Canterbury East.

20. Southern. After the 1923 Amalgamation there was a requirement for locomotives of greater power than that of either the L's or of the E1 and D1 Classes but which, at the same time, must be within the then axle load limit of $18\frac{1}{2}$ tons. In 1926, fifteen handsome locomotives of Class L1 appeared and were an immediate success, working the 80-minute Folkestone expresses with ease. They differed from the L's, mainly in having smaller cylinders but a higher working pressure. The cylinders and valves were re-designed and the piston valve travel was increased. As a result of experience with this class, engines of Class L were modified as they went through the shops and their performance greatly improved. Shown here is B.R. No. 31787 working a down Margate excursion train near Herne Bay.

21. L.M.S. The Midland, and then the L.M.S., were the only British Railways to use compound locomotives on a big scale after the Webb era on the London and North Western. In 1900 S. W. Johnson originated the design of a 3-cylinder compound 4—4—0 on the principles of William Smith, Chief Draughtsman of the North Eastern Railway. One inside high pressure cylinder and two outside low pressure cylinders were used. The design was developed by R. M. Deeley who designed a regulator valve by which the engines could always start as non compound with high pressure steam in the low pressure cylinders. On opening the regulator further, the "jockey valve" closed and the engines worked as compounds. During Henry Fowler's tenure of office as C.M.E. at Derby, all the forty-five Midland engines were superheated, and in L.M.S. days from 1924, another one hundred and ninety-five engines were built with 6ft 9in instead of 7ft 0in driving wheels. None of the Midland engines survived to be among "the Last Steam Locomotives" but a number of the L.M.S. engines did so.

Illustrated is L.M.S. No. 904, working in Scotland where the compounds did much of their best work. This engine had a Stanier chimney.

22. No. 1054 was piloted by Class 2 No. 545 on an express for Manchester awaiting departure from St. Pancras in 1938. This was a typical combination of motive power on the Midland line in pre-war days.

23. L.N.E. Prominent among modern 4—4—0s were H. N. Gresley's 3-cylinder D49 Class. Introduced in 1927 they had conjugate valve gear, but as the cylinders were three in line, this gear was fitted behind the cylinders instead of, as in Gresley's Pacifics, in front of them. Six engines were fitted with Lentz poppet valves with oscillating cams operated by Walschaerts gear. They were not very satisfactory and were altered to piston valves in 1938. The engines were named after British Shires and Counties and became known as the *Shire* Class.

No. 2760 WESTMORLAND, in immaculate condition, was photographed at Eastfield.

24. In 1929 Gresley equipped two of the *Shires* with rotary cam Lentz valves and when further engines of this class were built in 1932, they also had this form of steam distribution. The new engines were named after Hunts and the two altered *Shires* had their names changed to those of Hunts so that the whole series of rotary cam engines became known as the *Hunt* Class (D49/2). In 1949, two *Hunts*, Nos. 62763 and 62764, were experimentally fitted with Reidinger R.C. valve gear.

Shown is B.R. No. 62753 THE BELVOIR with an up slow train near York.

25. Southern. In 1930 R. E. L. Maunsell produced what will always be regarded as one of the most outstanding locomotive designs of all times as well as the most powerful 4—4—0 ever to run in Europe. Even more extraordinary was, that at a time when the 4—4—0 had almost universally been regarded as obsolete, the *Schools* Class should take over fast and important main line working on some of the busiest routes in the world. At one time these engines regularly worked 350-ton trains on a schedule of 116 minutes for 108 miles on less than a tank (4,000 gallons) of water. They were beautifully proportioned and had three sets of Walschaerts valve gear. The axle load of 21 tons could be accepted for all of the Southern main lines in view of the perfect balancing of the cranks set at 120°, and gave them a factor of adhesion of 3·75 for a tractive effort of 25,130 lb. The cab sides were sloped inwards so that the engines could run on the Hastings line with its restricted loading gauge.
B.R. No. 30902 WELLINGTON shows the fine appearance of these engines, officially known as Class V.

26. When O. V. S. Bulleid came to the Southern as C.M.E. in 1937 he was greatly impressed by the *Schools*. Many experiments in draughting and blast arrangements were in train at that period and experiments with the Lemaitre multiple jet blast pipe were carried out on the Class V engines. As a result twenty-one of the total class of the forty engines were fitted. Although these "big chimney *Schools*" had the reputation for particularly free running, the advantages were not considered great enough to equip the whole class.
B.R. No. 30938 ST. OLAVES is shown working an up boat express passing Ashford.

The 4—4—2 wheel arrangement originated in America in order to provide room for a wider fire box than could be accommodated on a 4—4—0 locomotive. Several experimental locomotives were built with this wheel arrangement in 1879–82 but it was not until 1894 that the design was firmly accepted in a series of locomotives for the Atlantic Coast Line. From this stemmed the name "Atlantic" by which the type has since been known.

In Britain, H. A. Ivatt designed the first Atlantic in 1898 for the Great Northern Railway. Rather surprisingly, no advantage was taken to provide a wide fire box in this design and No. 990 had a narrow box between the frames. However, after building ten more of this class and trying out a similar engine with four cylinders, Ivatt, in 1902 produced his " Large Atlantic " with an impressive boiler having a wide Wootton fire box which took full advantage to spread over the trailing wheels. Although the Large Atlantics were always good engines it was not until they were superheated and many given piston valves that they gave their brilliant best performances and became something of a locomotive legend.

Hot on the heels of Ivatt's original engines came, in 1899, the extraordinary Lancashire and Yorkshire inside cylinder Atlantics designed by J. A. F. Aspinall, with 7ft 3in driving wheels and a high-pitched Belpaire boiler.

The Great Western were next in the field and in 1903 and 1905 purchased three de Glehn compound Atlantics from the Société Alsacienne. During the next few years, in order to compare the merits of simple and compound machines, Swindon built a 4-cylinder simple 4—4—2 and thirteen 2-cylinder 4—4—2s after converting a 4—6—0 to a 4—4—2 in 1904.

The French engines remained as Atlantics but the other Great Western engines were all rebuilt as 4—6—0s.

Undoubtedly the most beautiful of all British 4—4—2s were J. G. Robinson's engines first built in 1903 for the Great Central Railway; in 1905 four more of these engines were built as 3-cylinder compounds on the Smith system.

Most impressive of British Atlantics were W. P. Reid's massive machines for the North British Railway introduced in 1906, though probably the last two, introduced in 1921 by W. Chalmers, and built with superheaters, were the most efficient in the stud.

The North Eastern completed the East Coast trio of companies to own 4—4—2s, with three basic classes—the first a 2-cylinder design of massive proportions designed by W. Worsdell in 1903 and known as Class V. Second were the most outstanding of the North Eastern Atlantics, the two 4-cylinder compounds designed by W. M. Smith, the Chief Draughtsman, and third came Vincent Raven's 3-cylinder Z Class in 1911, elegant and fast machines particularly in their superheated form.

Finally, the only other company to own Atlantics was the London, Brighton and South Coast which introduced two classes, the first Class H1, originally without superheaters, in 1905 and the second, Class H2, superheated and with larger cylinders, in 1911. The designer was D. E. Marsh who had worked on Ivatt's Large Atlantics at Doncaster. Small wonder then, that the Marsh engines bore a very strong resemblance to those of the Great Northern.

27. The only engines of the Atlantic type to survive long enough to be among the Last Steam Locomotives of British Railways were five of the L.B. and S.C. Class H2 and B.R. No. 32421 is shown here. It was B.R. Class 4P.

0—6—0

The first standard-gauge 0—6—0 engine to run in Britain, and indeed in the world, was probably constructed by Timothy Hackworth at Shildon in 1827 for the Stockton and Darlington Railway and named ROYAL GEORGE. It is possible that Hackworth's EXPERIMENT preceded it by a few months, but it is not proven whether or not this engine began life as an 0—6—0 or whether it was converted thus from an 0—4—0 at a later date.

The 0—6—0 formed by far the numerically largest type of steam locomotive to be used in Britain during the Age of Steam. It had the advantage that while all the engine weight was available for adhesion, the wheel base could be made short enough for it to negotiate all the curves found on main and secondary lines. The type was widely used on nearly all of the world's railways and at a time when in Britain it has nearly disappeared large numbers are still to be found at work in Europe and further afield.

Before the advent of the 4—4—0, the passenger locomotive counterpart of the 0—6—0 took the form of a six-wheeled engine which could be 2—2—2, 2—4—0 or 0—4—2, and boilers and other parts were frequently identical.

In its later history the 0—6—0 has proved to be the freight engine counterpart of the 4—4—0, and there are many instances of interchangeable boilers, cylinders and cabs among large groups of both types. Unlike the 4—4—0, the 0—6—0 type developed soon after its introduction as an inside-cylinder machine and there are very few instances of British 0—6—0s with outside cylinders.

This was quite contrary to European practice where, although the inside cylinder 0—6—0 was far from being unknown, the great majority of such engines had outside cylinders, and almost universally was this so in later practice. Holland and Belgium may be quoted as exceptions. Further afield and away from the spheres of British influence, the same pattern was evident.

A few railways used the 2-cylinder compound system especially during the latter part of the last century. The great advocate for compounding in this form was T. W. Worsdell who introduced it on the Great Eastern Railway in some 4—4—0 locomotives. When he went to the North Eastern Railway in 1885 he put into service no fewer than one hundred and seventy-one 0—6—0s of Class C which were inside cylinder 2-cylinder compounds on the Worsdell-von-Borries system. These engines formed by far the largest group of 2-cylinder compounds ever to run in Britain. His younger brother who succeeded him at Darlington, converted them all to 2-cylinder simples.

In Britain, the multi-cylinder 0—6—0 was almost unknown. In modern times there has been but one example—a 4-cylinder simple which was in 1924 rebuilt from an 0—6—0T built in 1922 for the North Staffordshire Railway, to the designs of J. A. Hookham.

This engine is of interest in that it had cranks set at 135° in relation to one another giving the engine eight exhaust beats for each revolution and ante-dating R. E. L. Maunsell's work on the Southern by several years. It was scrapped in 1928.

So the inside cylinder 0—6—0 reigned supreme. Most railways followed the same pattern in developing the type. The cylinders gave the clue. To start with, 17in × 24in or 26in provided different railways with hundreds of similar engines. 17½in × 26in, and 18in × 26in required little change in boiler size but the next step, 18½in or 19in × 26in was accompanied by much larger boilers, and tentatively at first, superheating. Finally, a pair of 20in diameter cylinders were about the largest which could be comfortably put between the frames and superheating and increased boiler pressures produced some very powerful machines. Coupled wheel diameters varied between 4ft 6in and 5ft 8in according to the duties required of the class. Many 0—6—0s were regarded as mixed traffic engines and engines with over 5ft 0in diameter wheels were commonly used on passenger duties by most railways. In fact, the only reason why many 0—6—0s were not used on passenger trains was because they were not fitted with continuous brakes, a wry comment on the old-fashioned and out-dated methods of freight operation in Britain

28. Great Western. Until the advent of the 2301 Class in 1883, most of the 0—6—0s for the Great Western Railway under the Armstrong regime had had double frames. With their single inside frames, William Dean's standard *Dean Goods*, therefore, were a complete break with tradition. No less than 280 were built between 1883 and 1899 and although only two or three survived to be among the Last Steam Locomotives, most of the class put in fifty years and more of hard and useful work. The first twenty engines were built with domeless round top boilers but after several transitional boiler changes, most of the class received domed Belpaire boilers, with from 1911 onwards, superheaters. Many *Dean Goods* were sent overseas in both World Wars and some ended their careers in far distant lands. There were slight variations in wheel diameter according to tyre thickness and some engines had cylinders 17½in instead of 17in diameter. In 1907 a start was made to convert twenty of them into 2—6—2T for the Birmingham suburban traffic.
The plate shows B.R. No. 2538.

29. L.N.E. No. 5090 was one of the 201 locomotives designed by T. W. Worsdell for the North Eastern Railway and built between 1886 and 1894. All but thirty were built as Worsdell-von-Borries 2-cylinder compounds but all were converted to simples before 1922. The compounds were Class C and the simples C1 but when all the engines became simples they were classified C (L.N.E. J21). Many were later superheated with piston valves and No. 5090 is one of these. They were excellent and economical all-round machines and were very popular with the men, especially on the trans-Pennine routes and for working excursion trains in the North East.

30. L.N.E. An excellent example of the "17in non-superheater 0—6—0" was the Great Eastern Class Y14 introduced in 1883 by T. W. Worsdell and which became L.N.E. Class J15. Some 290 of them were built, the last in 1913, and about 60 remained to be among the "Last of Steam". They were altered but little over the years. Many had pop safety valves, most were given bell-mouthed chimneys in place of the original stove pipes and a few had side-windowed cabs.

B.R. No. 65448 is shown working a local freight in the Colchester area, with the 25 kV catenary stretching out above her.

31. L.N.E. Between 1892 and 1902 the Great Central Railway built one hundred and twenty-four 18in 0—6—0 Goods engines with 5ft 1in wheels. They were of Classes 9D, 9H and 9M and the classes differed in the size of tender attached. They had Stephenson Link Motion instead of Joy's gear which had been fitted to previous 0—6—0s. T. Parker was the designer, though most of the engines were built in the time that Harry Pollitt was C.M.E. and the last were built during J. G. Robinson's tenure of office. They became L.N.E. Class J10 and B.R. No. 65148 is shown working freight on the Cheshire Lines. The hideous tapered "flower-pot" chimney fitted to these and other Great Central engines by H. N. Gresley, will be noted.

32. L.N.E. B.R. No. 65319 was North British Railway Class C, L.N.E. Class J36, the most numerous class on the N.B.R. with 168 engines. They were designed by M. Holmes and built between 1888 and 1890. Twenty-five went overseas during World War I and, on their return, were given names relevant to that war (e.g., FRENCH, MAUDE, VERDUN).

33. L.M.S. B.R. No. 57284 was one of 244 engines designed by Dugald Drummond for the Caledonian Railway and introduced in 1883. They were built over a period of 14 years, the design being modified and modernised by both Lambie and McIntosh and, finally, by the L.M.S. The original Drummond design had the safety valves on top of the dome.

34. L.M.S. No. 12053 was one of Barton Wright's tough little 0—6—0s introduced in 1887 and Class 25 on the Lancashire and Yorkshire Railway. They had slide valves placed between the cylinders and actuated by Stephenson Link Motion. Many of the earlier engines were converted to saddle-tanks by J. A. F. Aspinall (**Plate 251**).

35. L.M.S. The Midland Railway's locomotive policy was discussed on page 20 when dealing with the Johnson 4—4—0s and their derivatives. The Johnson Class 2 0—6—0s followed something of the same pattern of development but the story is much more involved since 906 were built between 1875 and 1902 including some for the Somerset and Dorset Joint Railway, and a few others for the Midland and Great Northern. The design was altered from time to time, driving wheels being either 4ft 11in or 5ft 3in diameter, and cylinders 18in or 18½in × 26in. Working pressure was either 160 p.s.i. or 175 p.s.i. and the engines never had superheaters. Originally, round-top boilers with Salter safety valves on the dome was the pattern and the photograph shows No. 3151 in this form. Some survived thus until after 1955.

36. From 1917 many of the Johnson 0—6—0s were modernised by rebuilding with Belpaire boiler, pop safety valves, a much larger cab and, in the case of B.R. No. 58119 shown here, a Stanier chimney. Under R. M. Deeley, a large number of the Johnson Class 2's were given much larger round-top non-superheater boilers and became Class 3. These engines are illustrated and discussed on page 38, **Plate 48.**

37. Southern. James Stirling was Locomotive Superintendent of the South Eastern Railway from 1878 until 1898. He came from the Glasgow and South Western Railway and his locomotives for both companies were characterised by domeless boilers. His first design for the South Eastern was an 0—6—0 which became Class O and of which 122 were built between 1878 and 1899. It is of interest to recall that the first engines had hand operated brakes on the tender wheels only, which contrasted strangely with more modern innovations such as a smokebox regulator and steam reverser. The typical Stirling rounded cab was also a feature of the design. Later engines had various modifications to frames and boilers and all were ultimately fitted with vacuum brakes. From 1903 H. S. Wainwright rebuilt the whole class with domed boilers and standard cabs, these engines being classified O1. It is in this form that No. 31425 was photographed at Dover.

38. The South Eastern and Chatham Railway came into being in 1899 and H. S. Wainwright was the Locomotive and Carriage Superintendent. His first locomotives for the new company were, perhaps his best and simplest design. The first C Class 0—6—0s appeared in 1900 and one hundred and nine were built during the period 1900—08. They had domed boilers, steam reversers and were never superheated. One of the class, No. 685 was converted to a saddle tank in 1917. Otherwise, no major alterations were made to the class. The C Class were exceptionally free running engines and were capable of working main line passenger trains at up to 70 m.p.h. when called upon to do so. In the 1930s they were commonly seen on the Kent Coast with 10 coach excursion trains bound for Margate. All save about 20 lasted into the Last Days of Steam.   The photograph of B.R. No. 31715 shows well their appearance.

39. Southern. B.R. 32440, Class C2X, was one of D. E. Marsh's 45 rebuilds of some of R. J. Billinton's standard C2 Goods engines for the London, Brighton and South Coast Railway. Rebuilding went on from 1908 to 1940 and mainly in providing new and much larger boilers and improved cabs, though the tractive effort remained the same. Six of the C2X Class, including No. 52440, were given top-feed domes; in Southern Railways days, however, this was no longer used though the dome remained.

39A. C2 Class, No. 452 shows the engine in its original form. Fifty-five were built between 1893 and 1902, but none lasted until 1955.

40. Southern. B.R. No. 30576 was designed by W. Adams for the London and South Western Railway. Between 1881 and 1886, seventy of these Class 395 engines were built and many of them served in Palestine and Mesopotamia in the First War. Latterly, they received frequent boiler changes and that on No. 30576 was of London Chatham and Dover origin.

41. Great Western. G. J. Churchward who was C.M.E. of the Great Western Railway from 1902 until 1921, designed no 0—6—0 tender engines, preferring 2—6—0s and 2—8—0s to deal with mixed traffic and heavy freight respectively. As the Armstrong 0—6—0s and later, the Dean Goods became obsolete, there was a requirement for further 0—6—0s on some of the company's secondary lines. Accordingly, in 1930 there appeared from Swindon No. 2251 to the designs of C. B. Collett, and between then and 1948 no fewer than 120 were built, the last one, No. 3219 being the first Swindon engine to be built there under B.R. "ownership". The 2251 Class had domeless tapered boilers and they were, of course, all superheated when built. They had commodious side-window cabs and, with a maximum axle loading of only $15\frac{3}{4}$ tons, they could work almost all over the system. They were frequently used on passenger duties and were very lively little engines with a good turn of speed.

B.R. No. 2211 was on slow passenger duty when photographed in Cornwall.

42. L.N.E. In 1908, H. A. Ivatt introduced on the Great Northern Railway, fifteen mixed traffic 0—6—0s of Class J21 (L.N.E. Class J1) with 5ft 8in wheels, and 18in × 26in cylinders. They had the same saturated boilers as his N1 Class 0—6—2T. In 1909 appeared Class J22 (L.N.E. Class J5) of which B.R. No. 65490 is an example. These twenty engines had 5ft 2in driving wheels but in all other respects they were identical with Class J21. A few were later superheated.

43. L.N.E. H. N. Gresley succeeded Ivatt in 1911 as C.M.E. of the Great Northern Railway, and the first engines to appear under his regime were further 5ft 2in 0—6—0s. Class J6 were fitted with superheaters, piston valves and cylinders 19in diameter. The boilers were identical with those of the Class D1 4—4—0s but the working pressure was 170 p.s.i. against 160 p.s.i. on the 4—4—0s. Between 1911 and 1922 one hundred and ten engines of Class J6 were built and the plate shows B.R. No. 64207, fitted with a tablet catcher, working a local freight at Lincoln.

44. L.N.E. Between 1901 and 1910 the Great Central Railway put into service 174 very handsome 0—6—0 locomotives of Class 9J (L.N.E. Class J11) to the design of J. G. Robinson. They had 5ft 2in driving wheels and 5ft diameter Belpaire boilers. The chimneys were beautiful and harmonious; the cabs comfortable and commodious. As a result of their mellow exhaust beat, they were known as the "Pom Poms". In 1909 one engine was built with 20in diameter cylinders and superheated. The boiler pressure was reduced from 180 p.s.i. to 160 p.s.i. After this, many of the class were superheated but retained their original cylinder diameter and working pressure. After the 1923 Amalgamation H. N. Gresley ruined their appearance by fitting them all with tapered "flowerpot" chimneys.

The plate shows B.R. No. 64280, superheated and with Gresley type chimney and snifting valve on a local freight near Sheffield.

45. From 1942, thirty-three of the Pom Poms were extensively rebuilt with long travel piston valves above the cylinders and with the superheated boiler pitched higher in consequence. B.R. No. 64394 is shown here.
It was at one time decided that these J11/3 locomotives should form a Standard Class on British Railways and a large number of new engines were scheduled. The idea, however, ultimately was abandoned.

46. L.N.E. Wilson Worsdell in 1890, succeeded his older brother T. W. Worsdell to become C.M.E. of the North Eastern Railway. In 1894 he introduced his Class P (L.N.E. Class J24) 0—6—0 for mineral working and in 1898 the larger and more powerful Class P1 (L.N.E. Class J25) of which No. 1970 is shown here. The boilers of the P1 were identical with those of the earlier Class C (**Plate 29**) but the cylinders had a longer stroke and the driving wheels were 4ft 7¼in diameter as against the 5ft 1¼in of the Class C. They had steam brakes only. Some engines of the class were superheated.
The later developments of the P Class are shown in **Plates 63 and 64.**

47. L.N.E. In 1906 W. P. Reid introduced on the North British Railway the first of 76 large 0—6—0 freight engines of N.B. Power Class B (L.N.E. Class J35), the design being a development of the smaller Holmes engines (**Plate 32**). Most of the engines were built with piston valves and saturated boilers though some of the later engines were given slide valves. With 5ft 0in diameter coupled wheels they were used frequently on secondary passenger duties. Sixty of the class were running at the end of 1955 and all had been superheated, the boilers being identical with those of L.N.E. Class J37 though pitched much lower. Shown here is B.R. No. 64516 with superheater boiler, working an up freight train south of Aberdeen.

48. L.M.S. The Class 2 Johnson 0—6—0s of the Midland Railway were described on page 23 (**Plates 35 and 36**). A number of the later engines of both the 4ft 11in and the 5ft 3in series were rebuilt with much larger round-top Class 3 boilers. From 1906 to 1908 R. M. Deeley built new at Derby, 70 identical engines with Class 3 boilers and 5ft 3in wheels. All the Class 3 engines were rebuilt with Belpaire boilers of the same diameter during Henry Fowler's term of office, but none was ever superheated.
B.R. No. 43244 is shown working a freight train down the Lickey Incline.

49. L.M.S. The Furness was one of Britain's smaller railways which none-the-less had a number of interesting locomotives during its history. W. F. Pettigrew was Locomotive Superintendent from 1897 to 1918 during which time he introduced a number of 0—6—0 freight engines some of which had variable blast pipes while others had Phoenix superheaters—later removed. The final series of 0—6—0 had 4ft 7½in coupled wheels, and round-top saturated boilers with extended smoke boxes. Four of them survived to be among the Last Steam Locomotives but they were all rebuilt with Lancashire and Yorkshire non-superheated Belpaire boilers with extended smokeboxes, and No. 12494 is shown in this state.

50. L.M.S. Among the best loved 0—6—0s, the Aspinall 27 Class of the Lancashire and Yorkshire Railway ranked high. Developed from the already well-tried Barton Wright 0—6—0s (**Plate 34**) they made their debut in 1889 with round-top boilers and 5ft 1in coupled wheels. B.R. No. 52455 is shown at Manchester Victoria. The last of the class were built in 1918, construction having been continued under the direction of H. A. Hoy and George Hughes. Four hundred and eighty-four were built during this period and inevitably there were variations, the most obvious being in the boilers. Saturated Belpaire boilers with extended smokeboxes (**Plate 49**) were fitted to many engines while some were superheated and retained their round-top boilers, twenty-two being so built in 1909 and later having the superheaters removed. In 1912, twenty were built with superheater Belpaire boilers and others were similarly rebuilt; the superheaters used in these engines were of three different types. **Plate 51** shows L.M.S. No. 12580 with Belpaire superheater boiler.

39

52. L.M.S. B.R. No. 57555 working a local freight southwards near Motherwell. This was one of 79 engines of the Caledonian 812 Class designed by McIntosh and built 1899–1900. The boilers were identical with those of the *Dunalastair I* Class and the cabs with those of the *Dunalastair II* Class. L.M.S. boilers were fitted to most of them but none was superheated. They were classed as mixed traffic engines but originally, only 16 were Westinghouse fitted and five had vacuum brakes. A further seventeen were built in 1908–9 and had *Dunalastair III* Class cabs, but were otherwise identical.

53. L.M.S. B.R. No. 57667 working freight on the Oban line. W. Pickersgill introduced his 0—6—0 locomotives in 1918 as a modern development of the McIntosh engines (**Plate 52**). The boilers, though higher pitched, were identical, wheels and cylinders of the same size. Piston valves, mechanical lubricators and snifting valves at the base of the smokebox formed part of the design though the locomotives were not superheated. From 1927 onwards, however, most of the class of 43 engines received superheaters.

54. Southern. On page 17 (**Plates 12 and 12A**) were described Dugald Drummond's T9 Class locomotives and their rebuilding by R. W. Urie. Two years before the T9's appeared, Drummond introduced, in 1897, his 700 Class 0—6—0s and thirty were built by Messrs. Dübs and Co., of Glasgow. The boilers, with safety valves on the dome, were identical with those of the M7 Class 0—4—4 Tank engines which were contemporary (**Plate 220**), and like the early batches of the M7's, the 700 Class had conical smokebox doors which were necessary to house some form of spark arrester in the smokebox. This was later removed and normal smokebox doors were fitted. For some now long-forgotten reason, the 700 Class were known as the "Black Motors".

In 1921, R. W. Urie decided to reconstruct the class to modern standards. Although much of the original boiler was used, a superheater was fitted together with an extended smokebox and the working pressure raised from 175 p.s.i. to 180 p.s.i. The boiler was pitched higher, the centre line being raised by 8in. Cylinder diameter was increased from 18½in to 19in but the slide valves were retained. The frames were lengthened by 18in at the front end to carry the larger smokebox.

B.R. No. 30352 is shown.

Plate 54A shows No. 306 in her original state except for the smokebox door.

55. L.N.E. B.R. No. 65503 Class J17 working freight near March.
Between 1900 and 1911 ninety 0—6—0 freight engines of Class G58 were built to the design of J. Holden for the Great Eastern Railway. The first batch had round-top boilers which were interchangeable with those of the early *Claud Hamilton* Class (page 15, **Plates 8 and 8A**). Later engines had larger Belpaire boilers which again were identical with those of the later *Claud Hamiltons* and with which all the engines were fitted. The whole class subsequently was superheated, and some were fitted with vacuum brakes for passenger train working. The L.N.E.R. classification was J17.

56. L.M.S. 0—6—0 superheated freight locomotive No. 58 of the Somerset and Dorset Joint Railway. This was one of five engines built for the S. & D. J. by the Midland Railway at Derby in 1922. It shows the original condition of the Midland Class 4 freight engines of which a description is given on page 43.

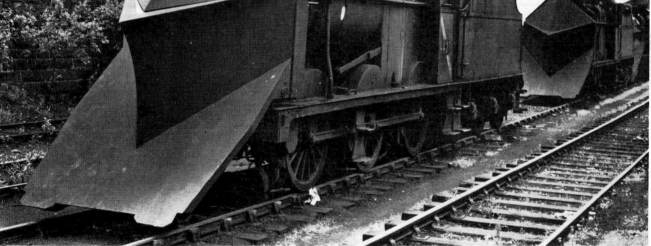

57 and 58. L.M.S. The Midland Superheated Class 4 0—6—0 was designed by Henry Fowler and first built in 1911. The design was changed hardly at all and it was accepted as a standard freight locomotive for the L.M.S. In all, 772 engines were built (including 5 for the S. & D. J. R. (**Plate 56**)) between 1911 and 1940. The Midland engines had right-hand drive, those of the L.M.S. left-hand. Like the Midland Class 2 4—4—0 (**Plate 16**) the Class 4 engines were probably economical machines but the design was a poor one, due mainly to their having insufficient bearing surfaces in the driving boxes which were far too small. It is still a matter for conjecture why so many should have been built without any alteration to improve the design. Although the Class 4 was frequently used for passenger train working its B.R. classification was only for freight.

The top picture shows one of the Midland engines B.R. No. 43937 with Stanier chimney working a Cromer to Birmingham ten-coach Saturday special train. The location was the Ouse Bridge at South Lynn on the former M. and G.N. line.

The lower picture shows L.M.S. built engine B.R. No. 44276 fitted with a snow plough and coal bunker cover for duty on the Leeds—Carlisle line.

59 and 60. Southern. R. E. L. Maunsell designed the Class Q freight engines to replace many older 0—6—0s which had lasted beyond their economic lives owing to their light axle loadings. With the great improvements in the Southern permanent way and structures, this condition was greatly reduced and the Q had an axle loading of 18 tons. The twenty engines went into traffic in 1938–9, actually after Maunsell's retirement. As originally built with single blast-pipes and chimneys they were poor steamers, the dimensions of the chimney not conforming to later formulae found to be basically correct and successful. Accordingly, after O. V. S. Bulleid had demonstrated the efficacy of the Lemaitre multiple jet blast-pipe for his own locomotives of Class Q1 (**Plate 68**), he successfully applied it to the Maunsell engines. In the course of much work on draughting carried out, mostly under the direction of S. O. Ell at Swindon, during the 1950s it was found that by the application of the formulae evolved, a better rate of steaming could be achieved by fitting the Q Class with the blast-pipe and chimney assembly of the B.R. Standard Class 4 2—6—4T. The project was also attractive as the maintenance of the Lemaitre blast-pipe was far heavier due to corrosion, than that of a single blast-pipe. Engine No. 30549 ran experimentally for a while with an unadorned stove pipe chimney and then a start was made to alter the engines back to single blast-pipes—a project which was not completed before the class was eliminated.

The top picture shows No. 533 as running soon after completion and with single (Maunsell) blast-pipe and chimney. It also had S.E. & C. type sniffing valves—one on each side of the smokebox.

In the lower view B.R. No. 30531 had a Lemaitre blast-pipe and the sniffing valves had been removed, when she was photographed working local freight at Hassocks. The steam reverser, with which all the engines were fitted, is clearly seen.

61. L.N.E. B.R. No. 64661 seen working freight at March was one of A. J. Hill's 25 large 0—6—0s built for the Great Eastern Railway between 1916 and 1920. They were G.E. Class T77 (L.N.E. Class J19) and originally had superheated Belpaire boilers interchangeable with those of the later *Claud Hamilton* 4—4—0s. The engines were almost identical with a series built in 1912 and G.E. Class E72 (L.N.E. Class J18). From 1934 all engines of Classes J18 and J19 were rebuilt with Gresley round-top boilers as applied to Class D16/3 (**Plate 8**).

62. L.N.E. B.R. No. 64681 on a local freight at Wickford. This was G.E. Class D81 (L.N.E. Class J20) designed by A. J. Hill and of which 25 were built 1920–22. They had Belpaire superheater boilers and until the building of the Southern Class Q1 in 1942, were the most powerful British 0—6—0s. The boiler and cylinders were standard with those of the 1500 Class 4—6—0s (**Plate 100A**). From 1943, all the J20's were rebuilt with round-top boilers identical with those with which the 1500 Class were also rebuilt (**Plate 100**). J20 No. 8280 was the first British locomotive to be fitted with Lentz O.C. poppet valves.

63. L.N.E. Plate 46 showed the 1898 development of the Class P1 freight engine. The next stage came in 1904 with Wilson Worsdell's Class P2 (L.N.E. Class J26). With wheels and cylinders of the same size as those of the P1, the P2 had an enormous saturated boiler of 5ft 6in diameter, no less than 15in more than that of the P1. The pressure was 200 p.s.i. but this was reduced to 180 p.s.i. Fifty engines were built and they remained in the forefront of North Eastern freight power for more than sixty years.   B.R. No. 65814 is shown.

64. L.N.E. The final development of the P Class came in 1906 with Class P3 (L.N.E. Class J27) which had deeper fireboxes and were built with 180 p.s.i. pressure. The last batch of 35 engines was built under the direction of Vincent Raven in 1921—23 who provided them with superheaters and piston valves; in later years, however, the superheaters were removed from 19 of these engines but the piston valves of course, retained. The total of P3 engines was 115.

The plate shows L.N.E. No. 2386, one of the superheated engines, working a freight train south of York.

65. L.N.E. As replacements for the many ageing 0—6—0 locomotives inherited by the new company in 1923, H. N. Gresley designed two classes of very powerful engines, both of which were put into traffic in 1926. The two classes had everything in common except that Class J39 had 5ft 2in coupled wheels and J38 4ft 8in, and that the boilers of the latter class were 6in longer than those of J39. The J39 Class numbered 289 engines which were built between 1926 and 1941. They were free running engines and were used in all classes of service all over the system. There were three parts to the class depending on the type of tender attached.

The plate shows B.R. No. 64882 with an express freight of perishables near March.

66. Class J38 actually appeared a few months before the J39's and there were only 35 of them built. With a tractive effort of 28,415 lb, they were the third most powerful British 0—6—0. They spent their entire lives in Scotland being used mostly for the heavy mineral traffic in the Fife coalfields, and for freight working to and from Leith and other docks.

B.R. No. 65914 is seen here at the head of a freight train about to leave Leith North.

67. L.N.E. The most powerful 0—6—0 ever built for a Scottish railway was the North British Railway's S Class (L.N.E. Class J37) which appeared in 1914 to the design of W. P. Reid, and over the next seven years, 104 were built. They were excellent machines and with their 5ft 0in coupled wheels were capable of working passenger trains upon occasion. They were frequently to be found on both passenger and freight duties on the West Highland line as well as on coal trains in Fife.
From the plate showing B.R. No. 64579 it will be seen that they were vacuum fitted.

68. Southern. B.R. No. 33015 Class Q1 the most powerful 0—6—0 design ever to run in Britain.
In response to an urgent wartime requirement for a powerful locomotive which could run over the whole system, O. V. S. Bulleid designed the Q1 which went into traffic in 1942. The engines were loudly publicised as an austerity design, shorn of all non essentials such as running plates, splashers and conventional boiler clothing, in order to save metal and other materials for the War effort. In point of fact the "austerity" was entirely due to the Civil Engineer who limited the engine's weight to 52 tons, a weight which Bulleid achieved with ¾ ton to spare. The boiler, however, was not stinted in any way and the firebox heating surface was 170 sq ft with a grate area of 27 sq ft. Working pressure was 230 p.s.i. and a five-jet Lemaitre blast-pipe and wide chimney were fitted. Long lap piston valves were placed above the cylinders and the coupled wheels were of cast steel. They were excellent machines despite their unconventional appearance. (W. A. Stanier on seeing one of them is reputed to have asked Bulleid, "Where do you wind it up?".) The Continental system of numbering was used for these engines before 1948, the engine number being prefixed by the capital C.

2—6—0 and 2—6—2

The first 2—6—0 tender locomotive in Britain was designed by William Adams and fifteen were built by Neilson and Co., and put into service on the Great Eastern Railway in 1878 after Adams had retired. They were very powerful machines and the first one was named MOGUL on account of this and remembering the Great Moguls of India. The name has been universally adopted for the type, though by no means have all subsequent Moguls been so powerful. All fifteen engines were scrapped by 1887, and the type was not reintroduced into Britain until 1895 when the Midland and South Western Junction Railway bought two from Beyer Peacock.

Next on the scene in 1899 were eighty 2—6—0s built in the United States by Baldwin for the Midland Railway who had forty, and the Great Northern and Great Central with twenty each. These engines had bar frames and bogie tenders but only lasted ten to fifteen years before being scrapped.

There followed, in 1901 the first of William Dean's 2—6—0s for the Great Western Railway. These engines known as the *Aberdare* Class had double frames for the coupled wheels but single inside frames, and bearings, for the leading truck. The Caledonian Railway (1912) and the Glasgow and South Western Railway (1915) each had a series of inside cylinder, inside framed 2—6—0s which were developments of existing 0—6—0 classes.

Although the 2—6—0 type is obviously a more satisfactory vehicle for mixed traffic duties involving higher speeds than is an 0—6—0, its development in Britain was surprisingly slow. Some authorities consider that this was due to the unfavourable aesthetic impact of the imported American machines of 1899. However this may be, it is certain that some locomotive engineers in the early years of the century were apt to refer to any 2—6—0 as a "damned Yankee design".

The 2—6—0 really came into its own when G. J. Churchward introduced his 4300 Class in 1911. Outside cylinders with piston valves, taper boilers, superheaters and many other features all made for a design which was " modern " forty years on. H. N. Gresley's Class K1 of 1912 and its larger boilered version of 1914 gave another boost to the type and Maunsell's Class N of 1917 for the South Eastern and Chatham Railway have never been bettered for their type and size. So the Mogul was established as a most useful and suitable type for mixed traffic duties in Britain. An interesting point is that all of the earlier 2—6—0 designs were described as " goods engines "—the description " mixed traffic " seldom appeared until much later on.

There is no need here to recount the later history of the type but mention must be made of the most remarkable of all British 2—6—0s, the 3-cylinder design of H. N. Gresley for the Great Northern Railway in 1920 and later classified K3 by the L.N.E.R. With a 6ft diameter boiler and a tractive effort of 30,000 lb. they were the first multi-cylinder 2—6—0s and were, at the time, among the giants of locomotive design. They proved capable of working 20-coach trains at speeds of up to 75 m.p.h. Small wonder then, that those interested in steam locomotive practice sat up and rubbed their eyes while a few of the more enlightened realised that a new era of great locomotive design was just commencing.

The 2—6—2, or Prairie, wheel arrangement was neglected by British designers and, in spite of its popularity overseas, there was only one example of its use as a tender engine in Britain until 1936. The one engine was an experimental 2—6—2 with eight single-acting trunk type cylinders. Steam distribution was by sleeve valves which could be rotated over ports in the cylinders to effect reversal of the engine. It was built at, of all places, conservative Derby, for the Midland Railway to the design of Cecil Paget, the General Superintendent of the Company. Its trials and even its existence were shrouded in the greatest secrecy and only in comparatively recent times have details of this interesting experiment been made known. It ran only a few times, failing mainly because of steam leakage between the sleeve valves and the cylinder liners. It was given the running number 2299 and its tender ran for many years behind Derby's other unusual design No. 2290—the "Lickey Banker" (**Plate 195**).

The next 2—6—2 to be built was H. N. Gresley's 3-cylinder Class V2 for the L.N.E.R., a very different proposition and one which provided the Company with one of the most useful and successful designs in steam locomotive history. After a further design for a smaller 3-cylinder engine also by Gresley, the 2—6—2 once again disappeared from the British Railway scene.

69 (Opposite, top). L.M.S. In its post-war assessment of the motive power requirements of a great railway, the London, Midland and Scottish Railway postulated that only eleven locomotive types would be required to deal with all traffic. High on the priority list was the need for small, modern and efficient engines for secondary and branch line services. This, in itself, was a partial break with the traditional idea that many such services could be worked by old main-line locomotives which had themselves been replaced by more modern machines. H. G. Ivatt designed two excellent locomotives for secondary services, one a 2—6—0 tender engine and the other its exact counterpart in the form of a 2—6—2 tank engine. (**Plate 290**.) Both engines were of Power Class 2 with a maximum axle load of 13 tons 11 cwt for the tender engine and 13¼ tons for the tank. Rocking grates, self emptying ashpans and manganese steel liners for horn guides and axle-box faces, were details of these essentially modern designs. One hundred and twenty-eight of the tender engines were built, about half of which had cylinders 16in × 24in while in the later engines the diameter was 16½in. The pleasing appearance of these locomotives is shown in the view of B.R. No. 46520.

70 (Opposite, below). B.R. No. 78030 Class 2 was one of a series of sixty-five locomotives introduced in 1953 and built under the direction of R. A. Riddles. They were basically identical with the L.M.S. Class 2 2—6—0s and they had their tank engine counterparts in the 84000 series 2—6—2T (**Plate 291**). As a result of the precipitate political dieselisation of British Railways from 1955 onwards, these locomotives were scrapped long before the expiry of their economic life.

71 (Above). B.R. No. 77009 Class 3 working empty stock at Glasgow Central Station. The Standard Class 3 2—6—0s formed one of the smallest classes of new engines, only twenty being built in 1954. They worked in Scotland and in North East England. The boilers were similar to the Swindon Standard No. 2 boiler as used on the Great Western 56XX series of 0—6—2T and others. The tank engine version of the Class 3 2—6—0 was the 2—6—2T of series 82000 which, in fact, were built in 1952, two years before the tender engines (**Plate 292**).

72. L.N.E. B.R. No. 61760 on a coal train near Sedgebrook. H. N. Gresley introduced the first ten 2—6—0s for the Great Northern Railway in 1912. They were Class H2 (L.N.E. Class K1), and with their raised running plates and outside Walschaerts gear they set the pattern for Great Northern (and L.N.E.) locomotive practice for many years to come. The engines were only a moderate success; with a boiler diameter of only 4ft 8in and two 20in × 26in cylinders they were decidedly under boilered. The fact was recognised and when the next engines appeared in 1914, Class H3 (L.N.E. Class K2), the boilers were 5ft 6in diameter and they were an immediate success. Ultimately all the K1's received larger boilers and they became Class K2. As they had inside steam pipes they were always distinguishable from the 1914 engines in which the steam pipes were outside. They were introduced during the Ragtime era and were known as ''Ragtimers'' for this reason. They were used all over the L.N.E.R. and became well loved on the West Highland line for which duties they were given cabs with side windows—and names.

73. B.R. No. 76044. One hundred and fifteen of these useful engines were built, the first appearing in 1953. Built to excellent modern standards under the direction of R. A. Riddles, and with an axle load of only 16¾ tons they were widely used and always highly regarded. They followed very closely the design of the L.M.S. Class 4 engines introduced by H. G. Ivatt (**Plates 74 and 75**).

74. L.M.S. When H. G. Ivatt put his new 2—6—0s into traffic in 1947 they were classified 4F although they were essentially mixed traffic engines. With cylinders, motion and pipe-work well exposed they were easy to maintain but were criticised aesthetically. The large double chimney certainly did nothing to help their appearance nor, as it turned out, their steaming capacity. After the work carried out on the test plant and by controlled road testing by the Swindon "team" a formula was evolved which, when applied to the engines, more than doubled the steam production of the boiler and enabled a single blast-pipe and chimney to be used. All the later engines of this class had single blast-pipes and the earlier engines were all suitably altered.

74 (Above) shows L.M.S. No. 3001 Class 4F as built.

75 (Below). B.R. No. 43104, Class 4MT as built with single blast-pipe, working a slow train between King's Lynn and Peterborough

78 (This page, above). Southern. The London, Brighton and South Coast Railway introduced the 2—6—0 type in 1913 with the powerful superheated locomotives of Class K designed by L. B. Billinton. They had 10in diameter inside admission piston valves actuated by inside Stephenson Link Motion, and were the first Brighton engines to have Belpaire boilers. Seventeen engines were built between 1913 and 1921 and after the Amalgamation they were modified by R. E. L. Maunsell with standard cabs and lower domes and chimneys to increase their route availability.

B.R. No. 32340 is seen at Brighton.

76 (Opposite, top) and 77 (Opposite, lower.) Great Western. G. J. Churchward designed no 0—6—0 locomotives, preferring for mixed traffic working the 2—6—0 wheel arrangement which, at that time 1911, was an unusual type for British railways. His 4300 Class were an unqualified success from the first and between 1911 and 1932, three hundred and forty-two were built. They were equally at home on freight or express passenger trains and have at times taken over such famous expresses as the Cornish Riviera in emergency. With two cylinders having 30in stroke they were inclined to impart a marked ''to and fro'' motion to the train, especially if running well ''notched up'' and they could, on occasion, roll quite alarmingly. Over the years, there were various modifications, different types of chimney, alterations in the frame length at the rear end and in the type of the motion-bar cross frames, were the most evident. As a result of excessive wear on the flanges of the leading coupled wheels when working on severely curved routes, an alteration in weight distribution was made to some engines in 1931 and a 30 cwt casting fixed behind the front buffer beam. The last twenty engines of 1932 were built with this modification. They also had side-window cabs and outside steam pipes. As the older engines became due for cylinder renewals, they too had outside steam pipes and **Plate 76** shows B.R. No. 6364 so modified. **Plate 77** shows one of the last batch, No. 9307 as she appeared when new.

79 (Top) and 80 (Lower). Southern. The great importance of the South Eastern and Chatham Railway's lines to the Kent Channel Ports during the First War required more powerful and modern locomotives than were then available. However, not until 1917 were materials available for R. E. L. Maunsell to build at Ashford the first of his Class N 2—6—0s No. 810. There was some similarity in the design to the Great Western 4300 Class (**Plate 76**), such as the taper boiler, the top feed (though of a different type) and the smokebox regulator, the last incorporated in Maunsell's excellently designed superheater. The long travel, 10in diameter piston valves were, however, actuated by outside Walschaerts valve gear and this, together with a raised running plate, made for good accessibility and ease of maintenance. Midland influence in this and other S.E. and C. designs, was seen in the shape of the smokebox and of the cab: Maunsell's Chief Draughtsman, James Clayton, was a former Derby man. No. 810 proved an excellent machine, but the war ended before the N Class could have any influence on traffic and it was not until 1920 that a further fifteen engines could be started at Ashford. The last engine of this series was built in 1923 with three cylinders and had H. Holcroft's conjugated valve gear. After the war, Woolwich Arsenal made complete sets of parts of the N Class design in order to keep the shops from closing down. Boilers, however, were made by the North British Locomotive Company. It was hoped by the Government that other railways would purchase these parts in order to replenish their locomotive stock. There were no takers! After the Grouping, in 1925, the Southern Railway purchased parts for fifty engines at a very cheap price, a further twenty-six sets of parts went to Irish Railways and six to the Metropolitan Railway who built them into 2—6—4 tank engines. Eighty Class N engines were built between 1917 and 1932, the final eight having left-hand drive. In 1930, No. A819 became the subject for steam conservation trials which lasted for five years after which the pumps, condensors and square chimney with which it had been fitted, were removed. The Class N engines were to be found all over the system—equally at home on the steep gradients of Devon and Cornwall as hauling coal trains from the Kent mines or working express trains to the Kent Coast.

Plate 79 shows B.R. No. 31407, one of the left-hand drive engines, working the up Thanet Belle composed of ten Pullmans and the crack Kent Coast train in the days of steam.

Plate 80 shows B.R. No. 31848 with right-hand drive and rebuilt with new cylinders having outside steam pipes. This design modification dated from 1955, about half being dealt with before the elimination of the class. Smoke deflectors were fitted from 1933 but No. 31848 was without them, for a time after her cylinder renewal.

81A and 83A. Southern. The Class K 2—6—4 tank locomotives were designed soon after Maunsell became C.M.E. of the South Eastern and Chatham Railway in 1913. As a result of the First War, however, it was not until 1917 that the first engine No. 790 was completed to enter traffic contemporaneously with the first N Class. The K was, in fact, a tank engine version of the N with 6ft 0in diameter coupled wheels in place of 5ft 6in. In 1925–26 in Southern Railway days, a further twenty engines were built one of which No. 890 had three cylinders with Holcroft's conjugated valve gear. The engines were named after rivers and Southern No. A804 RIVER TAMAR is the subject of **Plate 81A (above)** while the 3-cylinder Class K1 No. A890 RIVER FROME is shown in **Plate 83A (below).** As a result of several derailments of the *River* Class at high speed on poor track culminating in the Sevenoaks disaster of 1927 all the Class were converted to un-named 2—6—0 tender engines of Class U (**Plate 81**) and thirty projected K Class were built new as Class U, although this decision had been made prior to the accident (**Plate 82**). The 3-cylinder engine when rebuilt became Class U1.

81. Southern. B.R. No. 31807 Class U, on a Salisbury to Portsmouth Harbour train leaving Southampton Central. This engine was one of the converted K Class tank engines which differed from the new Class U in having deeper splashers and lower running plates.

82. Southern. B.R. No. 31621 one of the new Class U is here shown with cylinders having outside steam pipes, a modification carried out from 1955 when new cylinders were required (Cf. Class N).
One of the Class U engines No. A629, in 1929 was equipped to burn pulverised fuel. No advantage was found and the engine reverted to normal in 1932.

83. Southern. Class U1, B.R. No. 31906 on a down Kent Coast express near Herne Bay. In 1931 20 U1's were built with three sets of Walschaerts gear instead of the conjugated valve gear of the first one No. A890 which was itself altered thus in 1932. The U1's put in some of their best work on the Kent Coast service.

84. Class N1, B.R. No. 31876. No. A822 (B.R. No. 31822) with Holcroft's valve gear was the only N1 until 1930 when five more were built with three sets of Walschaerts gear; No. 822 was altered to this design in 1931. Although used mainly on the Hastings line, N1's were quite capable of timing the business expresses between Cannon Street and Ramsgate.

85. L.M.S. B.R. No. 42880. George Hughes, former C.M.E. of the Lancashire and Yorkshire Railway, became first C.M.E. of the London Midland and Scottish Railway in 1923. His main contribution to L.M.S. motive power was the "Horwich Crab" which appeared in 1926 after Hughes had retired and of which 245 were built. They were excellent modern mixed traffic engines with long lap, long travel valves and adequate bearings. The angling of the cylinders was necessary in order to keep the dimensions within the Midland loading gauge.

86. Five of Hughes' 2—6—0s were, in 1931, given new cylinders and Lentz R.C. poppet valve gear with no advantage over the piston valve engines accruing. In 1953 these engines were equipped with Reidinger gear, shown here, and which was inferior to both other forms of steam distribution.

87. L.M.S. B.R. No. 42954 working freight near Oxford. These 2—6—0s were W. A. Stanier's first main-line engines for the London Midland and Scottish Railway after becoming C.M.E. in 1932. The first one appeared in 1933 with a Great Western type of cover to the top-feed. This was promptly removed and replaced by the dome-shaped cover seen here. Forty engines were built with smokebox regulator valves and small super heaters. Subsequently, all had 21-element superheaters. It was found possible to locate the cylinders horizontally by making them 18in × 28in and with a W.P. of 225 p.s.i. to obtain the same tractive effort as that of the Hughes design which had cylinders 21in × 26in and W.P. 180 p.s.i.

88 and 89. L.N.E. The appearance in March 1920 of H. N. Gresley's Class H3 (L.N.E. Class K3) No. 1000 for the Great Northern Railway caused a sensation in railway circles, amateur and professional alike. It carried the largest diameter (6ft) boiler ever put on to a British locomotive; it was the first 2—6—0 ever to have 3-cylinders; it was the first 3-cylinder locomotive to have Gresley's "two-to-one" conjugated valve gear as modified by Holcroft from Gresley's original and patented design in 1915 (and applied to his first 3-cylinder 2—8—0); it had coupling and connecting rods made of high tensile, but highly resonant, nickel chrome steel which magnified the characteristic "Gresley knock" into an even more characteristic ringing "clank". Although the cabs were of the rather short and uncomfortable Great Northern pattern a great effort had been made to make the fittings and controls easy of access and regulator handles were arranged at each side of the cab while the screw reverser was designed to work vertically instead of horizontally. Ten engines were built before the 1923 Amalgamation.

Plate 88 shows L.N.E. No. 4003 in its original state though not with its Great Northern tender. After 1923, a further one hundred and eighty-five engines were built, the last appearing in 1937. Some modifications in springing and weight distribution were made but the most obvious development was the reduction in height of boiler mountings to suit the Scottish loading gauge, and the provision of double-window cabs. Various tenders were affixed. The original engines later received large cabs and lower chimneys and domes.

Plate 89 depicts B.R. No. E1844, filthy, grimy and with cylinder head covers missing, working a coal train from Peterborough to London near Potters Bar.

90 (Above). L.N.E. B.R. No. 61998 MACLEOD OF MACLEOD Class K4. Mention has already been made (page 52) of the fact that some of H. N. Gresley's early 2-cylinder 2—6—0s worked successfully on the difficult West Highland line in Scotland. In 1937 Gresley introduced his 3-cylinder Class K4 locomotive designed especially for the West Highland and named LOCH LONG. With cylinders $18\frac{1}{2}$in × 26in (as in the Class K3) but with only 5ft 2in wheels it was nominally the most powerful of the L.N.E.R. Moguls with a tractive effort of 36,600 lb. The boiler, however, was only 5ft 6in in diameter and the total heating surface was less than that of the K2 boiler. The explanation was that on the West Highland, long sustained boiler output at high speeds was not required; the requirement was for a free-steaming boiler capable of high output for short periods at low speed. Conjugate valve gear, placed ahead of the cylinders, was used and the engine was so successful that five more of the class were built in 1938–9.

Edward Thompson who succeeded Gresley as C.M.E. of the London and North Eastern Railway in 1941 is reputed to have had a strong dislike of "all things Gresley". Be this true or not, he certainly took a very different view of locomotive design, taking a generally more simple and straightforward but much less sophisticated approach. In the difficult war years during which he held office, it was obviously impossible to make many fundamental design changes and most that were made may be seen as simplification for the future when standards of locomotive maintenance were likely to be, and indeed were, deplorably low compared with the pre-war years. Thus three cylinders were to be abandoned in favour of two in all except the Pacifics, a policy which got rid of the most hated Gresley feature, the conjugated valve gear. In the event, only two engines of the 2—6—0s were altered to two cylinders before Thompson retired in 1946.

Plate 91 (Opposite, top). L.N.E. B.R. No. 61863, Class K5 was Thompson's rebuild with two cylinders of Gresley's 3-cylinder Class K3 (**Plate 89**). One engine only.

Plate 92 (Opposite, middle). L.N.E. B.R. No. 61997 MAC CAILIN MOR on an express passenger train on the West Highland line. This was Class K1/1, Thompson's 2-cylinder rebuild of Gresley's 3-cylinder Class K4 (**Plate 90**). One engine only.

Plate 93 (Opposite, lower) .B.R. No. 62056, Class K1. This was A. H. Peppercorn's 1949 development of Class K1/1. Seventy were built. The frames were a little longer and the total weight slightly less than those of the rebuild, and there were other small differences. They were widely used especially in the East and North East, as well as in Scotland.

94. L.N.E. B.R. No. 60821 working freight south of Peterborough.

H. N. Gresley designed the first of this country's 3-cylinder 2—6—2s for the London and North Eastern Railway. The first engine appeared in 1936 and was named GREEN ARROW to coincide with the introduction of a special fast freight service of the same name. The boiler was the same as that for the Class A3 Pacific (**Plate 150**) but the barrel was 1ft shorter. The three cylinders, steam chests and smokebox saddle were made in one casting with short outside steam pipes. Gresley's conjugated valve gear placed ahead of the cylinders, was used to drive the middle valve. The leading pony truck of the swing-link type had 5½in deflection each side of centre, while the trailing carrying wheels had 2½in, being fitted with Cartazzi radial axleboxes. Some modification was made to this arrangement following the derailment of one of the V2 engines at Hatfield in 1946.

95. Class V2, No. 813 on a down Leeds express leaving Potters Bar tunnel.

The Class V2 engines were always able to produce adequate steam for their needs. After the war, however, the "self-cleaning smokebox" came increasingly into use and this involves an arrangement of plates and wire mesh in the smokebox which deflect the cinders, char and hot fire-box gases, at first downwards and forwards and then upwards and backwards through a wire screen and into the chimney petticoat. The large cinders are broken up by the wire screen and pass through it to the chimney and out to atmosphere. This system naturally produces some resistance to the flow of gases and effects steaming. No. 813 was fitted with modified chimney dimensions to overcome the difficulty and ran with a "stove pipe" during and after the experiments. The other engines of the class were altered but retained their conventional outer chimneys.

96. L.N.E. B.R. No. 60950 with long outside steam pipes.

As engines of the Class V2 became due for cylinder renewals it was found much more economical to do away with the large single casting for the three cylinders, steam chests and smokebox saddle. Instead, separate castings were made for the outside cylinders and steam chests which were then bolted on to the centre casting. Longer and more direct outside steam pipes formed part of the modification.

97. B.R. No. 60963. As part of a further series of draughting investigations carried out at Swindon the engine illustrated above was fitted with double blast pipe and chimney. No great advantage was obtained over the modified single blast pipe (**Plate 95**) which had overcome all the problems of steaming due to the fitting of self-cleaning apparatus. Of the class of 184 engines only six ever received the double blast pipe arrangement.

E

98 and 99. L.N.E. H. N. Gresley's final design for the London and North Eastern Railway was a 3-cylinder 2—6—2 with a maximum axle load of 17 tons, and a tractive effort of 27,420 lb. Thus the Class V4 was a powerful machine with a very wide route availability. As a result of the war and then the designer's death in 1941 only two of the class were built. The second engine differed in several ways from the first, most importantly in having a welded steel firebox with a single Nicholson thermic syphon in place of the conventional copper firebox. Both engines had Gresley's conjugated valve gear placed in front of the cylinders. After their initial trials, the V4 engines spent their lives in Scotland, mostly working on the West Highland line, and the plates show No. 1700 BANTAM COCK at work on this line. The second engine was never named.

The 4—6—0 became more highly developed in Great Britain than anywhere else in the world. During the last forty years it became the most widely used type for mixed traffic and express passenger duties, with coupled wheels of from 5ft 0in to 6ft 9in diameter.

The first 4—6—0 was a goods engine put into service in 1894 by David Jones for the Highland Railway. Fifteen were built by Sharp Stewart without any prototype trials. They had outside cylinders 20in × 26in with inside Allan Link Motion and 5ft 3½in coupled wheels, the driving wheels being originally flangeless.

During the next decade the 4—6—0 was adopted by several companies and developed both as an inside, and as an outside cylinder type. The Caledonian, for example, started with a neat inside cylinder mixed traffic engine with 5ft 0in coupled wheels for service on the Oban line. Other famous inside cylinder 4—6—0s followed: Caledonian *Cardean* Class, London and North Western *Experiment* and *Prince of Wales* Classes, Great Eastern 1500 Class and the Great Central *Sir Sam Fay*, this last with 21½in diameter cylinders, the largest ever put between frames. (The mixed traffic *Glenalmond* Class had the same size but in both classes they were later reduced to 20in.) The best of these inside cylinder engines were probably the Great Eastern 1500 Class as rebuilt by H. N. Gresley.

The greatest design progress was made in the outside cylinder type which became the usual 4—6—0 form. Before his retirement from the Highland, David Jones prepared an express engine design with 5ft 9in coupled wheels, an enlarged version of the " Jones Goods ". Named after Castles, they successfully went into service in 1900 under the superintendency of Peter Drummond, younger brother of Dugald. In 1911, the North British Locomotive Company built fifty of them for service on the French State Railway.

The North Eastern Railway was an early user of the outside cylinder 4—6—0 with its Class S designed by Wilson Worsdell. These engines had 6ft 1¼in wheels and were claimed as the first express passenger 4—6—0s. They were followed by Class S1 of 1901 with 6ft 8in wheels and later by Class S2, a larger 1919 version of the original S Class.

Some rather similar engines were built by J. G. Robinson for the Great Central, starting with two fine looking engines with 6ft 9in coupled wheels in 1903. Similar engines with 6ft 7in, 6ft 1in and 5ft 8in wheels followed.

In 1903, James Manson put into service on the Glasgow and South Western Railway, seventeen non-superheater 4—6—0s of which the less said the better. However, 1911 saw the introduction of two more engines with superheaters, piston valves and other improvements which more than restored Manson's reputation with his enginemen.

It was, however, on the Great Western Railway under the direction of G. J. Churchward that the greatest progress was made with the 4—6—0 having two outside cylinders. The fullest use was made of the type which began in 1902, and developed with little modification to culminate in the *Halls*, *Granges* and *Manors* of recent times. F. W. Hawksworth's *County* Class was the ultimate Great Western 2-cylinder 4—6—0, and which broke with the Churchward traditional design in many important details.

On the Southern, R. E. L. Maunsell's *King Arthur* Class were outstandingly successful express engines which owed much to Swindon in their conception.

The modern outside cylinder 4—6—0 found its best expression in the large numbers of mixed traffic engines in B.R. Power Class 5, any design of which was capable of a large range of duties previously undertaken by several different types.

The specially British development, however, was the non-compound multi-cylinder 4—6—0. Apart from a few of Webb's engines on the London and North Western, and the conversion of one of Hughes' L.M.S. 4-cylinder 4—6—0s to compound working, the compound 4—6—0 was unknown in Britain.

The first 4-cylinder simple engines were G. J. Churchward's *Star* Class for the Great Western, and these were developed and enlarged to the famous *Castle* Class of 1923 and the *Kings* of 1927—the most powerful 4—6—0 in Britain.

Some very poor 4-cylinder engines for the London and South Western in 1907 and 1911 were followed in 1908 by George Hughes' Lancashire and Yorkshire engines which had to be reconstructed before becoming successful. In 1913 Bowen Cooke introduced the *Claughtons* on the London and North Western, engines which gave more headaches to more mechanical engineers than any other class. Robinson's six 4-cylinder Great Central engines appeared during 1917-20 and were beautiful, as usual. The mixed traffic engines of 1921-4 with smaller wheels, were much more satisfactory.

Except on the Great Western, all the later designs of multi-cylinder 4—6—0s in Britain have had three cylinders and as they all lasted in one form or another to be among the Last Steam Locomotives, they are described elsewhere in this book. One class which did not survive and which was one of the most outstanding failures of all time, was William Pickersgill's 1921 design for the Caledonian Railway. Four engines only were built and they had Walschaerts valve gear for the outside valves and a most complicated form of derived gear to the inside valve. But the design was a bad one in many ways and not even the replacement of the inside valve gear by independent Stephenson Link Motion made much improvement in their performances.

100

100A

100 and 100A. L.N.E. The 4—6—0 locomotive designed by S. D. Holden for the Great Eastern Railway entered traffic in 1911 as Class S69 (L.N.E. Class B12) and were the last inside cylinder 4—6—0s to remain in service on British Railways. Seventy-one were built originally, a further ten being added by the L.N.E.R. in 1928. As built they had 5ft 1in diameter Belpaire boilers and, except the last ten, short travel piston valves. **Plate 100A** shows the prototype engine in its original form. In 1926 one engine was fitted with Lentz O.C. poppet valves and the last ten engines were built new with this form of steam distribution. They also had raised running plates above the coupled wheels. Between 1927 and 1934 many engines were given A.C.F.I. feed-water pumps and heaters. During, and after, the Second War a number of the B12's were sent north to Great North of Scotland territory, and they did fine work. Those engines which went north were mostly rebuilt with round-top boilers of the same diameter as the original Belpaire boilers. From 1932 H. N. Gresley started rebuilding the entire class with 5ft 6in diameter round-top boilers and long travel piston valves, a process considerably delayed by the war, but ultimately completed.

Plate 100 shows one of these engines, known as Class B12/3 at work on the L.N.E. main line between Grantham and Peterborough.

101. L.N.E.R. The need for a more powerful engine than the B12 Class for the Great Eastern main line was the reason for H. N. Gresley introducing the B17 Class in 1928. In view of their even torque, consequent upon the use of three cylinders, the adhesive weight of 54 tons—10 tons more than the B12—was accepted by the Civil Engineer. Unlike Gresley's other 3-cylinder designs the B17 had divided drive, the inside cylinder driving the leading coupled axle and the two outside cylinders, the second. As a result of this layout, it was possible to use the conjugated valve gear behind, instead of in front of the cylinders thus avoiding disadvantages arising from expansion of the valve spindles. The engines were named after famous houses, SANDRINGHAM being the first, and giving its name to the class. Further locomotives were built, notably for use on the Great Central line and later engines were named after Football Clubs. In all, seventy-three engines were built, of which, in 1937, two were streamlined, in the same manner as the Class A4 Pacifics and were used for the East Anglian Express London to Norwich. No. 2821 HATFIELD HOUSE is shown when new. Some engines were later rebuilt with 100A boilers as fitted to the Class B1 engines (Class B17/6).

102. Starting in 1945 Edward Thompson rebuilt ten B17s to Class B2 having two cylinders and 100A boilers. Shown is No. 1671 ROYAL SOVEREIGN maintained as the Royal Engine but here seen working an up Cambridge slow train.

103

103A

103 and 103A. Southern. The London, Brighton and South Coast Railway was never much more than an outer suburban railway and was therefore considered to be a most suitable terrain for tank locomotives. Many very handsome machines were built and the summit of Brighton tank engine design was reached in L. B. Billinton's two handsome 4—6—4T of 1914 known as Class L. Delayed by the war, a further five engines were put into service in 1921–2. Southern Railway No. 2328 is shown in **Plate 103A.** For several reasons, the 4—6—4 main line tank engine was not successful, although four companies built the type. Between 1934 and 1936 R. E. L. Maunsell rebuilt the seven Brighton L Class into 4—6—0 tender engines known as Class N15X and named the first six after famous locomotive engineers. The last engine retained its tank-engine name REMEMBRANCE as a memorial to L.B.S.C. railwaymen killed in the First War.

Plate 103 shows B.R. No. 32328 HACKWORTH.

104 (Top) and 105 (Lower). The British Railways Standard Class 4 for mixed traffic totalled eighty engines which were built at Swindon in 1951. With a maximum axle-load of $17\frac{1}{4}$ tons they had a high route availability and proved themselves to be lively and powerful little engines. They were the first standard type to be built with plain bearings with manganese steel liners instead of roller bearings.

Plate 104 shows No. 75034 leaving Bletchley with a slow train for Oxford.

In their original form, the Class 4 4—6—0s could produce enough steam (19,600 lb. per hour) for the duties they were called upon to perform, but it was often necessary, especially on the Southern Region, to work these engines very hard. As a result of trials carried out at Swindon under the direction of S. O. Ell, it was found that a suitably dimensioned double blast pipe and chimney enabled the steaming capacity of the boiler to be raised to 22,490 lb. per hour. From 1957 a number of engines were so fitted, including all those allocated to the Southern Region and one of these, No. 75074 is shown in **Plate 105.**

106. Great Western. Only three of G. J. Churchward's 4-cylinder 4—6—0s of the 4000 or *Star* Class survived to be among the Last Steam Locomotives.

B.R. No. 4062 MALMESBURY ABBEY was one of them. She had elbow steam pipes to new inside cylinders, the outside cylinders not having been renewed. Those *Stars* which had new outside cylinders had outside steam pipes similar to those of the *Castle* Class locomotives (**Plate 145**). No. 4062 was one of the last batch of twelve built in 1922—3 and all named after Abbeys. The class was introduced in 1906 and the first engine to appear was a 4—4—2, later converted to 4—6—0 (see page 18) ; this engine was also built with a "scissors" form of valve gear, but all other Great Western 4-cylinder engines had two sets of Walschaerts valve gear inside the frames, the outside valves being driven through rocking shafts. C. B. Collett's *Castle* Class and later the *Kings* were all developments of the original Churchward engines and not until after nationalisation was any major change introduced in the form of higher superheat and double blast pipes and chimneys.

107. Great Western. As a result of a requirement for a mixed traffic locomotive with better characteristics as a vehicle at high speeds than the 4300 Class 2—6—0 and with greater boiler power, C. B. Collett in 1924 rebuilt one of Churchward's 2-cylinder *Saint* Class with 6ft 0in coupled wheels. This engine, No. 2925 SAINT MARTIN (subsequently numbered 4900) became the forerunner of a class of 330 engines. Apart from the alteration in the diameter of the coupled wheels from the original 6ft 8½in, and the provision of a side windowed cab, no changes of importance were made to SAINT MARTIN. In 1948 the engine was given new cylinders with outside steam pipes.

108. Great Western. After SAINT MARTIN, the next engines of the *Hall* Class were a series of eighty built 1928–30. They differed from the prototype in having $4\frac{1}{4}$in higher pitched boilers, modified frames and cylinders with outside steam pipes. A further one hundred and seventy-eight engines were built, with only minor differences, until 1943. They were excellent and useful engines quite able to work all classes of trains except the heaviest freight. Like so many Great Western engines with two cylinders having 30in stroke, they could impart an uncomfortable to and fro movement in the train especially when running well notched up. B.R. No. 6927 LILFORD HALL is shown.

109. B.R. No. 6967 WILLESLEY HALL was one of the last seventy-one engines of the *Hall* Class which were known as the *Modified Halls* or as the 6959 Class. They were built between 1944 and 1950. The frames were built up entirely of welded plate as also were the bogie frames. Other changes were new pattern cylinders with longer outside steam pipes and 3-row superheaters providing 52 sq ft more superheater heating surface.

110. Great Western. B.R. No. 6861 CRYNANT GRANGE passing over Aynho Troughs while working an excursion train for Pwllheli. Eighty engines of the 6800 or *Grange* Class were built between 1936 and 1939 to the design of C. B. Collett as replacements for a similar number of 4300 Class 2—6—0s which were withdrawn and their wheels and motion used for the new engines. Owing to their having an axle load of 18 tons 8 cwt—4 cwt more than that of the 4300's, they did not have such a high route availability and were in fact a small-wheeled version of the *Hall* Class. None the less they were very useful engines covering a wide range of duties.

111. B.R. No. 7806 COCKINGTON MANOR. The 7800 or *Manor* Class were also built to replace 4300 Class engines and they received wheels and motion from withdrawn 2—6—0 engines. Twenty were built in 1938 and a further ten in 1950. To provide a locomotive "to go anywhere on the system" the axle loading was only $17\frac{1}{4}$ tons. This was achieved mainly by producing a smaller boiler but the tractive effort was only 1,500 lb less than that of the *Granges*. They were much more effective machines after having new chimneys fitted after 1953 as a result of tests carried out at Swindon. The *Manors* were used extensively in Cornwall and on the Cambrian lines.

112 (Top) and 113 (Lower). L.N.E. Edward Thompson's first new design for the London and North Eastern Railway was a 4—6—0 mixed traffic engine which appeared in 1942. As a result of the difficulties of war production it was 1944 before the first ten engines were completed at Darlington Works. Originally Class B they were reclassified B1 and ultimately four hundred and ten engines were built, many by outside contractors. A number of the engines were named after the various classes of antelopes while others carried the names of Directors of the Company but most were unnamed. In some measure, the B1 became to the L.N.E.R. what the *Black Stanier* Class 5 was to the L.M.S., though numerically the B1 had only about half the strength. Class B1 was a simple and straightforward 2-cylinder design with long travel long lap valves of 10in diameter. The boiler was similar to the type 100 boiler with 200 p.s.i. pressure fitted to the B17 class but had slightly different dimensions including larger grate area, and the higher working pressure of 225 p.s.i. No important modifications were made to Class B1 which did much useful work all over the system, and like the Class 5 L.M.S. engines, were popular in Scotland.

Plate 112 shows L.N.E.R. No. 1065 unnamed.

Plate 113 shows B.R. No. 61244 STRANG STEEL at work in Scotland.

114. L.N.E. B.R. No. 61456, Class B16/1 on a down freight train leaving York.
Between 1920 and 1923, Vincent Raven put into service on the North Eastern Railway seventy 3-cylinder mixed traffic locomotives of Class S3 (L.N.E. Class B16). They had three sets of Stephenson motion driving outside admission piston valves and the drive from all three cylinders was on the leading coupled axle. Coupled wheels were 5ft 8in diameter and the boilers were interchangeable with those of the Class T3 0—8—0s. They were good engines in their day, and as well able to cope with the Scarborough excursion traffic as to deal with heavily loaded fast freight.

115. L.N.E. B.R. No. 61475, Class B16/2.
In 1937, H. N. Gresley rebuilt one of the North Eastern Class S3 engines with new cylinders, inside admission piston valves above the cylinders, two sets of Walschaerts gear and with his conjugated valve gear for the middle cylinder placed behind the cylinders. Nickel chrome steel was used for connecting rods. The new boilers were of the same dimensions as the former ones, but a longer smokebox was fitted. Seven engines were rebuilt thus, and were Class B16/2, the unrebuilt engines becoming B16/1. From 1944, Edward Thompson rebuilt a further seventeen engines but he employed three sets of Walschaerts valve gear instead of using conjugated gear to the middle valve. These engines were Class B16/3

76

116 (Top) and 117 (Lower). L.M.S. In the history of British Steam Locomotive practice no locomotives have ever been so universally popular as W. A. Stanier's mixed traffic 4—6—0s of Class 5 (or more exactly, 5P5F). Equally at home on express passenger or heavy freight trains they averaged better than 150,000 miles between each general repair while their records of "hot boxes" and hot big ends were among the lowest ever known. All of which adds up to good design and excellent proportions. Two cylinders, outside Walschaerts gear, tapered boilers with top feed, and correctly dimensioned chimney and blast pipe, all were essential factors in the success of the class which first went into traffic in 1934. The first seventy engines followed Great Western practice and had domeless boilers and low temperature superheat with 14-element superheaters. No. 5005 of this first batch is shown in **Plate 116**. The next three hundred and seventy-seven engines of 1935-7 had boilers with larger grates, more firebox heating surface and 24-element superheaters. The regulator was in the dome and the top feed on the second ring of the boiler. Engines built after 1938 had 28-element superheaters and the top feed was on the first ring of the boiler. Later, much interchange of boilers occurred and **Plate 117** shows B.R. No. 45082 of the second batch of engines carrying a boiler of the third type and working an express, northwards from Leeds.

118 L.M.S. After the war and until 1951 a number of trials were conducted with new Stanier Class 5's. Roller bearings were found advantageous especially because they needed less maintenance. Double blast pipes and chimneys gave only marginal advantage when fitted either to piston valve engines or to those with Caprotti valves which were introduced in 1948. Little advantage was found with these engines over the piston valve engines, except that the enclosed design of the rotary valve gear was attractive from a maintenance point of view. B.R. No. 44741 with single blast pipe and Caprotti valves is the subject of **Plate 118.**

119. The final modification of the Stanier Class 5 was made under the direction of H. G. Ivatt after nationalisation, in 1951. Two engines were built with an improved form of Caprotti valve gear, double blast pipes and chimneys, Skefko roller bearings to all axles and raised running plates. B.R. No. 44687 is shown in **Plate 119.** The pipe leading down from the left hand side of the dome in the Caprotti engines admitted steam to the under sides of the poppet valves when the regulator was opened. This steam tended to keep the valves firmly in contact with the cams. When the regulator was closed the valves dropped back on to their bottom seatings leaving the ports wide open to produce a by-pass effect.

120 (Top) and 121 (Lower). L.M.S. One of the most noteworthy experimental modifications carried out on the L.M.S. Class 5 4—6—0s, was the building in 1947 of No. 44767 with piston valves actuated by two sets of outside Stephenson Link Motion, each using two return cranks instead of the usual two eccentrics. The purpose of this experiment was to see what real advantage accrued from having variable lead. A characteristic of Stephenson Link Motion is that the lead is increased by notching-up and this should be of benefit when running at high speeds with short cut-offs as the maximum possible amount of steam is enabled to enter the cylinder. No results from this experiment were published. (Although outside Stephenson Motion is commonly used on the Continent on quite modern locomotives, its previous application in this country was to a single driver express locomotive of the Great Western Railway in 1884.) The appearance of B.R. No. 44767 is shown in **Plate 120** while **Plate 121** shows the valve gear. This engine was also fitted with Timken roller bearings to all axles, manganese steel liners to axlebox guides, double blast pipe and chimney, self-cleaning smokebox, rocking grate and electric lighting.

The total number of Stanier Class 5 locomotives reached 842 in 1951 after which no more were built.

122. Southern. R. W. Urie was C.M.E. of the London and South Western Railway from 1912 until 1922, after which the company became part of the Southern Railway. During his ten years of office he brought the locomotive stock of the L.S.W. up-to-date particularly by his introduction of a series of ten strongly built and powerful 4—6—0 mixed traffic engines of which the first came out in 1913 as Class H15, Nos. 482–491. Even as late as 1913 the obvious advantage of superheating was not universally accepted and two of the class were built without superheaters. Ultimately, Urie equipped them with his own design of superheater. In 1927, R. E. L. Maunsell rebuilt one of the engines, No. 491, with a N15 (*King Arthur*) Class boiler, but the rest of this series retained their original boilers. **Plate 122** shows No. 488 as running in Southern days with Maunsell type superheater and snifting valves on the sides of the smokebox.

123. Class H15 was composed of four "parts" of very different engines having little more in common than the size of their cylinders (21in × 28in) and coupled wheels (6ft 0in). In 1915 Urie rebuilt extensively No. 335, a Drummond 4-cylinder engine of Class E14. The rebuild had two cylinders but retained the original boiler shell. In 1924, R. E. L. Maunsell rebuilt a further five Drummond 4-cylinder engines, Nos. 330–334 of Class F13 on similar lines but with detail differences. Also in 1924, Maunsell introduced his own version of the H15 with straight footplating above the cylinders and with an N15 Class boiler. Ten engines, Nos. 473–478, and 521–524 were built and **Plate 123** shows B.R. No. 30474 working a slow train from Southampton Central Station.

124 (Above). Southern. In 1920 Urie introduced a series of twenty 2-cylinder 4—6—0 locomotives of Class S15 with bogie tenders and designated for fast goods traffic. In fact, they often worked as mixed traffic engines though their coupled wheels were 5ft 7in—5in less than those of Class H15. The boilers were the same as those of Urie's N15 Class. As built they had stove-pipe chimneys but were later fitted with the shapely Maunsell chimneys.

In **Plate 124** B.R. No. 30507 is seen working a down freight near Brookwood.

125. Southern. No. 835 with 6-wheeled tender for the Brighton line. This was one of R. E. L. Maunsell's Class S15, with 200 p.s.i. pressure and 20½in × 28in cylinders. Fifteen were built in 1927 and a further ten in 1936 making a total of forty-five in the entire class. Boilers and motion were interchangeable with those of the Maunsell N15 Class.

F

126. Southern. 4—6—0 No. 453, Class N15 KING ARTHUR with an early form of smoke deflector plates.

After the 1923 Amalgamation, the Southern Railway was faced with greatly increasing passenger traffic and with insufficient locomotives to do the job. Furthermore, the Urie N15 or 736 Class 4—6—0s were proving quite incapable of reliable time keeping even with existing trains. R. E. L. Maunsell was planning a large express engine capable of taking 500 ton trains at 55 m.p.h. between London and Exeter. As this locomotive could not possibly be ready for several years, Maunsell and his energetic assistants set about replacing (or, officially, rebuilding) ten Drummond 4-cylinder 4—6—0s of Class G14, Nos. 448–457, by modern 2-cylinder engines with partly coned boilers, and well designed cylinders and steam chests with long travel piston valves and outside steam pipes. The bogie tenders of the Drummond engines were used and the new engines took the same numbers. The engines were named after the Knights of the Round Table and the first engine to appear in 1925, No. 453, became KING ARTHUR and so gave its name to one of the most famous and successful series of express locomotives in railway history.

At the same time the twenty Urie N15's of 1918–23 were tested exhaustively and by fitting to them the better proportioned chimneys and blast pipes of the Maunsell engine, their steaming capacity was brought up to the standards of the new engines. Without further major alteration, the Urie engines were able to take their places and their names in the ranks of the *King Arthurs*. They could be distinguished by having inside steam pipes and by their Drummond/Urie safety valves. **Plate 127** shows No. 755 THE RED KNIGHT as later fitted by Bulleid with a Lemaitre multiple-jet blast pipe and wide chimney.

More express engines were required for the 1925 services than the thirty N15's described above. So, an order for thirty engines was awarded to the North British Locomotive Company who delivered the first in May 1925. These engines Nos. 763–792 had modified cabs as fitted to Maunsell's South Eastern and Chatham engines, and could run over the Kentish lines. The bogie tenders were of the Urie type. These N15's were universally well-liked. (See **Plate 128,** opposite.) The last series of fourteen engines, making seventy-four in all, came from Eastleigh in 1926–7 and were built with 6-wheeled tenders for working on the Brighton lines.

128. Southern. B.R. 30764 SIR GAWAIN, Class N15, one of the "Scotch Arthurs" with an up Kent Coast express near Teynham.

129. B.R. No. 73086 THE GREEN KNIGHT, Class 5.

The British Railways Standard Class 5 locomotives were built under the direction of R. A. Riddles and appeared in 1951. Generally, they followed the design of the Stanier Class 5's (page 69) and the boilers were nearly identical. The cabs were of B.R. standard design and the footplate was supported by the boiler. The design of the cross-head, slide bars and motion followed that of the *Britannia* Class Pacifics and became standard B.R. practice. The vertical grid-type regulator in the dome was actuated by external rodding from a regulator handle of the "fore and aft" type. Twenty of these engines took the names of scrapped *King Arthur* Class engines, but the idea never made any impact on the travelling public.

130. B.R. No. 73089 at work on the Kent Coast with a down Ramsgate express. The "Standard Fives" did some of their best work in Kent taking over many services from worn-out N15's.

131. B.R. No. 73137 with Caprotti valves, leaving St. Pancras with a fast train for Leicester. Thirty engines of the one hundred and seventy-two standard Class 5 had British Caprotti valves and gear of the latest type. This gave good steam distribution with no back pressure and was mechanically efficient. As a totally enclosed unit it had considerable maintenance advantages over piston valves. It is likely that, had more steam engines been built, many would have had Caprotti gear. The similarity of No. 73137 to No. 44687 (**Plate 119**) may be noted, but all the standard Class 5's had most carefully proportioned single chimneys and blast pipes which were capable of producing maximum boiler output.

132 Great Western. F. W. Hawksworth's thirty *County* or 1000 Class of 1945–7 were the "ultimate" 2-cylinder 4—6—0s of the Great Western. Many of their features were new to Swindon practice; for example, the very high boiler pressure of 280 p.s.i., the straight splashers, the driving wheel diameter of 6ft 3in. and the double chimney and blast pipe which were fitted to the first of the class. The axle load of 19 tons 14 cwt made them essentially main line engines and they worked through to Penzance. The *County's* never achieved the popularity of other Great Western classes, most enginemen preferring the *Halls* and even the *Granges*. **Plate 132** shows B.R. No. 1015 COUNTY OF GLOUCESTER in its original form.

133 The Standard No. 15 boiler fitted to the *County* Class required more draught, proportionately, for a given output of steam than did other boilers as fitted, for example, to the *Hall* and *Grange* Classes. In their original form the performance of the *County's* left much to be desired, and they came under investigation by the Swindon experts on draughting and chimney design. As a result, from 1955 all the class was fitted with double chimneys and blast pipes having different dimensions from those with which the first engine was fitted. Their boiler output and consequently their performance, was greatly improved. **Plate 133** shows B.R. No. 1014 COUNTY OF GLAMORGAN working a Plymouth to Manchester express near Stapleton Road.

134A. L.M.S. At the 1923 Amalgamation and in the years which immediately followed, the London, Midland and Scottish Railway's main line was dependant for its top motive power on a comparatively few 4-cylinder 4—6—0s of Hughes' Lancashire and Yorkshire design and upon the 130 *Claughton* Class 4-cylinder 4—6—0s of Bowen Cooke's 1913 design for the London and North Western Railway. L.M.S. No. 6018 PRIVATE W. WOOD, V.C., is shown here. They were poor performers, with many bad design features and very expensive to maintain. After the *Royal Scots* (**Plate 137A**) had, from 1927, taken over the most important main line duties, attention was given to rebuilding or replacing the *Claughtons*. Many things had been done to try to improve them including the fitting of Caprotti valves to some and the rebuilding in 1928 of twenty with much larger (5ft 5½in diameter) boilers. In 1930, two engines were completely reconstructed with three cylinders having three sets of Walschaerts gear, long travel valves and large boilers of the 1928 design. Only the driving wheels remained of the old engines. These engines were entirely successful and became known, and loved, as the "Baby Scots" though officially they were the *Patriot* Class. All pretence of "rebuilding" was now dropped and the North British Locomotive Company built fifty to replace the *Claughtons* in 1934. Some carried the names of the engines they replaced.

Plate 134 (Lower). shows B.R. No. 45506 THE ROYAL PIONEER CORPS.

135. L.M.S. B.R. No. 45526 MORECAMBE AND HEYSHAM, Class 7P with an up express leaving Bletchley. As a result of the successful rebuilding in 1942 of two of the Stanier Class 5X engines with large taper boilers having 250 p.s.i. pressure and with double blast pipes and chimneys, H. G. Ivatt commenced a similar rebuilding of eighteen of the *Patriot* Class in 1946. The three cylinders were renewed and their diameters reduced from 18in to 17in. The rebuilt engines were always considered at least the equal of the rebuilt *Royal Scots* (**Plate 137**) and were much better riding engines.

Plate 136 shows B.R. No. 45532 ILLUSTRIOUS (left) alongside reboilered *Royal Scot* Class B.R. No. 46143 THE SOUTH STAFFORDSHIRE REGIMENT. The detail differences can be noted.

137A. L.M.S. Built in a hurry to solve an urgent traffic problem, the *Royal Scot* Class was designed at Derby under the direction of Henry Fowler and with much help from the Southern Railway and the North British Locomotive Company, who built the first fifty. They were very successful engines though always rough riders. Three cylinders were provided with three sets of Walschaerts gear and the slightly tapered boiler was 5ft 9in maximum diameter. As built they had vacuum pumps driven from the L.H. cross-head and brakes to the bogie wheels. The overall impression of power was marred by the small 3,500 gallon Midland tender.

137B. This shows the ROYAL SCOT on her return from a successful visit to America and Canada in 1933. (Actually the engine was No. 6152 renumbered 6100 for the tour.) Many detail improvements were made to this engine and ultimately to all the class, by W. A. Stanier, among them the provision of larger 4,000 gallon tenders.

138A. Experiments with very high pressure steam and compounding were carried out in Germany, U.S.A. and elsewhere. In 1929, the North British Locomotive Company built a modified *Royal Scot* No. 6399 FURY with Schmidt type very high pressure boiler. The engine was a 3-cylinder compound. While on trial near Carstairs a boiler tube exploded killing the driver and grievously scalding the fireman and a locomotive inspector, and the experiment was terminated. (See **Plate 138,** opposite.)

137. L.M.S. The final metamorphosis of the *Royal Scots* began in 1943 when No. 6103 was extensively rebuilt with re-designed cylinders and valves, and with a taper boiler and double blast pipe and chimney. The original type cab was, however, retained. The boiler was identical with those used on the rebuilt *Jubilee* Class engines, and was 12ft 11$\frac{1}{16}$in between tube plates. All of the seventy *Royal Scots* were ultimately rebuilt and became one of the finest large 4—6—0s ever known. They were still inclined to be rough riding engines, especially as they were getting run down, but their ability to steam, to pull and to run was never challenged. Although the rebuilding was doubtless inspired by Stanier it was carried out under the direction of C. E. Fairburn.

Plate 137 shows B.R. No. 46135 THE EAST LANCASHIRE REGIMENT with an eleven-coach down express climbing Shap without banking assistance.

138. W. A. Stanier rebuilt the ill-fated FURY in 1935 with three simple cylinders and a taper boiler. This was the first such boiler to be put on a *Royal Scot* and it was not very successful, the engine often being short of steam. It is probable that, in view of the success of later and much shorter taper boilers, the distance between tube plates of 13ft 9$\frac{3}{4}$in was too great. The engine, which became No. 6170 BRITISH LEGION, was later fitted with a double blast pipe and chimney which greatly improved the steaming. It is shown here in its original rebuilt form. (See **Plate 138A,** opposite.)

139. L.M.S. Without any extensive prototype trials, one hundred and thirteen 3-cylinder 4—6—0 express engines designed by W. A. Stanier were ordered in 1933, and ultimately one hundred and ninety were built. The engines were intended to be an improved, taper boilered, version of the *Patriot* Class. They had small superheaters and domeless boilers like the original Class 5's, and the first of the class, No. 5552, when new in 1934, is shown here. Unlike the Class 5, they were an immediate disappointment. They were usually short of steam and the low temperature superheat robbed them of much of the "vivacity" of the *Patriots*. In 1935 No. 5642 exchanged numbers with No. 5552 and was finished in black enamel with cast, chromium-plated letters and numerals, and chromium-plated dome cover and cleading bands. She was named SILVER JUBILEE and gave the name to the class.

140. Extensive trials showed that suitable alterations to blast pipe and chimney dimensions greatly improved the steaming capacity of the boiler while later engines were built with regulators in the dome, larger superheaters and bigger grates. All the earlier engines later received these improved boilers.
B.R. No. 45569 TASMANIA with the later type of boiler, is seen working the southbound Thames—Clyde Express from Leeds.

141. L.M.S. As well as the alterations made to the single blast pipe arrangements of the *Jubilee* Class, double blast pipes and chimneys were tried on two of the engines. As these were designed and fitted before the work on draughting had been carried out at Swindon, the results showed little improvement on the modified single blast pipes.
One of these locomotives, B.R. No. 45742 CONNAUGHT is shown working an up express from Windermere.

142. L.M.S. Even with the modifications already mentioned, war-time maintenance and poor coal found the *Jubilees* still in trouble for steam on occasions. New taper boilers based on the design of that fitted to No. 6170 (**Plate 138**) but with shorter barrels and other improved proportions, were fitted to two engines, No. 5735 COMET (shown here) and No. 5736 PHOENIX. Double blast pipes and chimneys and new 17in × 26in cylinders, completed the job and ended the steaming difficulties as far as they were concerned. This boiler was later applied to the *Royal Scots* (**Plate 137**), and to some of the *Patriots* (**Plate 136**) but, strangely enough, no more of the *Jubilees* were altered.

143A. Southern. After two years work on the design, R. E. L. Maunsell's 4-cylinder 4—6—0 No. E850 LORD NELSON went into service in 1926, as the locomotive which was to be capable of working 500-ton trains at 55 m.p.h. average on the Southern main line to Exeter. By using special high tensile steel for rods and motion and by obtaining nearly perfect balancing by setting the four cranks "off the quarters" it was possible to produce within the Southern's stringent weight restrictions, a locomotive with 33,500 lb tractive effort and an axle load of 20 ton 13 cwt. In 1926, No. E850 was Britain's most powerful express locomotive and subsequently fifteen more were built. Four sets of Walschaerts gear were provided, the inside cylinders driving the leading coupled axle and the outside cylinders, the second. The setting of the cranks gave eight exhaust beats to each revolution of the driving wheels.
Plate 143A shows No. E850 passing Sevenoaks with an up boat train.

143. The *Nelsons* were not very successful and never freely cleared their exhaust. When O. V. Bulleid became C.M.E. in 1937 he rebuilt them with new cylinders, 10in piston valves and Lemaitre multiple-jet blast pipes. Thus, when twelve years old, the *Nelsons* at last came into their own and gave the performance expected of their size and power. B.R. No. 30857 LORD HOWE as rebuilt by Bulleid, is the subject of the plate above.

144A. Southern. In 1936, with a future Pacific design in mind, Maunsell rebuilt No. 857 LORD HOWE with a large round-top boiler with a combustion chamber. The boiler plates were of nickel steel. The engine is shown after being rebuilt again by Bulleid with new cylinders and Lemaitre blast pipe. This boiler was subsequently replaced by a standard *Nelson* boiler (**Plate 143**).

144. Several major modifications were carried out by Maunsell to try to improve the *Nelsons* : (1) No. 865 had a new crank axle so that the cranks were at 90° to each other and gave four instead of eight beats to the revolution. (2) No. 860 was given a 10in longer boiler barrel—this was the intended design originally, but to economise. the standard *Nelson* boiler had the same length barrel as that of the *King Arthurs*, 14ft 2in between tube plates. (3) No. 862 was fitted with a Kylchap blast pipe. None of these gave any real improvement. (4) No. 859 LORD HOOD was given coupled wheels 6ft 3in instead of 6ft 7in diameter in order better to cope with the Dover Boat trains. This engine, as B.R. No. 30859 is shown in **Plate 144**. The change in wheels made no difference at all to its performance.

145. Great Western. B.R. No. 5058 EARL OF CLANCARTY (*Castle*) Class leaving Paddington with the Cheltenham Spa Express.

C. B. Collett's 4073 (*Castle*) Class 4-cylinder 4—6—0 was the logical development in 1923 of Churchward's 4000 Class (**Plate 106**). Fifteen of the latter as well as Churchward's only Pacific, were rebuilt as *Castles* but the frames of these engines did not always stand up to the increased power output. Between 1923 and 1950, one hundred and fifty-five *Castles* were built new. They were among the finest engines ever known in Britain and they greatly influenced locomotive design on the other three main-line companies. The inside cylinders drove the leading coupled axles, the outside cylinders, the second. Two sets of Walschaerts gear inside the frames drove the inside valves and the outside valves through rocking shafts. The original engines built up to June 1939, had 2-row low temperature superheaters as standardised by Churchward.

146. B.R. No. 7008 SWANSEA CASTLE with double blast pipe and chimney, 4-row superheater and mechanical lubricators. The forty *Castles* built after the War under the direction of F. W. Hawksworth were modernised by increasing greatly the superheat. During 1956, investigation at Swindon showed that suitably dimensioned double blast pipes and chimneys greatly increased the boiler output and also helped the engines to steam better on available coal which was greatly inferior to Welsh coal for which they were designed. About twenty engines were dealt with, and a number of the older ones received 3 or 4-row superheaters.

147.   Great Western. In 1927, Britain's most powerful express locomotive up to that time, appeared in the form of C. B. Collett's 6000 (*King*) Class. They were never greatly exceeded in tractive effort except by Gresley's rebuilt 4—6—4. With a maximum axle-load of 22½ tons and 6ft 6in coupled wheels they were essentially for the heaviest main line work and were confined to the London–Plymouth (both routes) and the London–Wolverhampton via Bicester, lines. As a result of their limited route availability, only thirty were built and they did all that was asked of them for the next thirty-five years.

The general layout followed that of the preceding 4-cylinder 4—6—0s, but smaller wheels and larger cylinders resulted in the bogie having its leading axle in an outside frame in order to clear the cylinders. A derailment at Newbury in 1927 resulted in some modifications being made to this unusual bogie.

Plate 147 shows B.R. No. 6025 KING HENRY III with an up Penzance express passing Teignmouth.

148.   Three events of importance stand out in the lives of the *Kings*. First, was the visit of No. 6000 KING GEORGE V to America in 1927 for the Baltimore and Ohio Centenary. A highly successful tour, one small result of which was the (alleged) Anglicisation of the appearance of three B and O engines. Second was the breakaway from G.W. tradition by the fitting, from 1947, of 4-row high temperature superheaters and mechanical lubricators and, third, the extensive 1953 Swindon Performance and Efficiency tests which included Controlled Road Testing with 21-car trains at express train timings. As a result it was found that by fitting properly dimensioned double blast pipes and chimneys the hourly rate of steam production could be greatly increased, and all the *Kings* were so modified.

B.R. No. 6029 KING EDWARD VIII is shown with double chimney and 4-row superheater.

4—6—2

The first 4—6—2 locomotive was built in America in 1902 for the Missouri Pacific Railway and it was from this source that the type received its name, Pacific.

The first European Pacific was a 4-cylinder de Glehn compound, built in 1907 by the Société Alsacienne for the Paris-Orleans Railway.

The first British Pacific was a 4-cylinder simple, built by the Great Western Railway in 1908 to the designs of G. J. Churchward who, however, never liked the engine and once said that it was built only as a prestige symbol to keep up with the French. It was named THE GREAT BEAR, numbered 111 and had driving wheels, cylinders and valve gear identical with those of the *Star* Class. With an axle load of 20½ tons and a wheelbase of 34ft 6in it was able to run only on the main line between Paddington and Bristol. THE GREAT BEAR was withdrawn in 1924 and replaced by a *Castle* Class engine No. 111 VISCOUNT CHURCHILL.

After being early in the field with the new type, the railways of Britain built no more Pacifics until 1922 and at a time when the leading European railways were using 4—6—2s for express work and 2—8—2s as the mixed traffic counterpart, Britain was content with 4—6—0s, 4—4—0s and 0—6—0s.

In 1922, H. N. Gresley introduced the first two of his 3-cylinder Pacifics for the Great Northern Railway and these engines and their L.N.E.R. successors are described later in this section. Also in 1922, Vincent Raven's North Eastern Pacific appeared, Class 4.6.2. (L.N.E. Class A2) and it went into service in 1923. No. 2400 and her four sisters, were massive machines with three cylinders all driving the leading coupled axle on which were also mounted the eccentrics for the three sets of Stephenson Link Motion—not perhaps, a very good arrangement, but one which had proved satisfactory on the Z Class Atlantics and on the S3 Class 4—6—0s of which the Pacifics seemed to be an enlarged version. The wheelbase was 40ft 5in and the boiler barrel 26ft 0in long but as there was a firebox combustion chamber and the front tube plate was set well back, the tubes were only 21ft 0in long. None the less, the class were never reliable steamers and even the fitting of a Gresley boiler to one of them in 1929 did not give much improvement. The first two engines of the class had inside radial axleboxes for the trailing wheels while in the last three the axleboxes were outside. All five engines were scrapped in 1937–8.

W. A. Stanier's first Pacifics for the London Midland and Scottish Railway were completed in 1933 and are described later. They, and Stanier's later Pacifics were all 4-cylinder simple engines except No. 6202 which was an experimental non-condensing turbine-driven locomotive known as the "Turbomotive". Boiler, wheels and much of the framing were standard with those of the *Princess Royal* Class but the drive was to the leading coupled axle through treble reduction gearing from a multi-stage steam turbine developing 2,000 h.p. and situated on the forward part of the left-hand side of the locomotive. A smaller turbine on the right-hand side was used for backwards running and by the use of a dog clutch this turbine could be engaged to the gear train through an extra reduction gear. Notwithstanding this quadruple reduction for backwards running, insufficient power was developed to assist the station pilot at Euston in lifting the empty stock back up Camden incline and a Class 8 freight engine had to be provided for the job.

This courageous and sound piece of experimental engineering threw up many problems and there were a number of failures and breakdowns all of which confirmed that the inefficient, rugged Stephenson engine had no betters in the realm of steam railway locomotion. Nevertheless, Stanier's "Turbomotive" was probably the most successful break-away from that concept of all time. The "Turbomotive" was withdrawn in 1952 and reconstructed as a 4-cylinder engine, B.R. No. 46202 PRINCESS ANNE.

PRINCESS ANNE was different from the other Class 8P Pacifics of both Stanier and Ivatt design. The "Turbomotive" boiler, standard with those of the *Princess Royal* Class, was retained, but the smoke box was 6in longer. The layout of cylinders, steam chests and steam pipes followed that of the *Coronation* Class, the cylinders being placed further forward than in the *Princess Royals*. The running plate dropped 3in backwards from the trailing coupled wheel. This engine had a single blast pipe and chimney and no smoke deflector plates. No. 46202 had a tragically short life being damaged beyond repair in the accident at Harrow and Wealdstone on 8th October, 1952, only a few weeks after being built at Crewe.

O. V. Bulleid's remarkable Pacifics for the Southern Railway made a sensational war-time debut in 1941 and so three of the four railway companies of Britain were well provided with powerful Pacifics which were to prove with one single exception to be the largest type of express steam locomotive to be used. By a strange irony the Great Western which had introduced the type ended up as the only company which did not own Pacific locomotives.

After nationalisation the first ever 2-cylinder British 4—6—2s were built, as well as a single 3-cylinder engine, officially to replace PRINCESS ANNE; but all these locomotives were among the last steam locomotives and as such are described in the pages which follow.

149A. Great Northern. H. N. Gresley's 3-cylinder 4—6—2 went into traffic on the Great Northern Railway in 1922 and the plate shows No. 1470 GREAT NORTHERN at Doncaster Shed, soon after her introduction. With a sister engine No. 1471 she became Class A1 on the L.N.E.R. Gresley's Pacifics, although expected as a logical development from the Ivatt Atlantics, none the less caused sensation and great interest when they arrived—the first of the type since the one and only Great Western Pacific of 1908. They had nothing in common with THE GREAT BEAR, and the wheelbase of 35ft 9in caused no worries except that it demanded a rather gentle approach to Kings Cross. Outstanding features were the large taper boiler 6ft 5in at its greatest diameter, and a grate area of $41\frac{1}{4}$ sq ft which caused enquiry as to whether one fireman could fire the engine. Three cylinders all driving the second coupled axle had valves operated by two sets of Walschaerts gear outside, the centre valve being driven by Gresley's conjugated valve gear in front of the cylinders as on the Class K3 Moguls. The coupling, piston and connecting rods were of (highly resonant) nickel chromium steel which for a weight reduction of 25 per cent had a breaking strength under test of nearly double that of normal carbon steel.

Gresley's bogie, good weight distribution and the Cartazzi radial wheels combined to make the engines excellent vehicles, and all Gresley's Pacifics rode magnificently. The cab was large and commodious and for the first time in British locomotive history the enginemen were provided with padded seats. With all this modernity, it was strange indeed that the valves should be of the short lap, short travel type of 8in diameter, which necessitated the engines being driven "on the regulator" and resulted in coal consumptions normally in excess of 50 lb per mile.

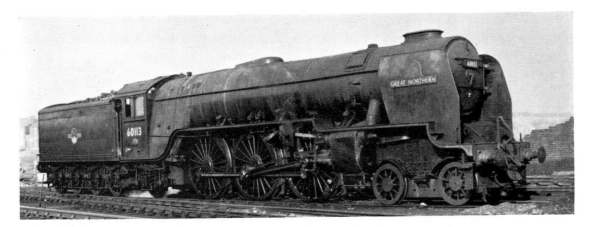

149. L.N.E. When Edward Thompson succeeded Gresley in 1941 he rebuilt GREAT NORTHERN completely in 1945. An A4 boiler, with double blast pipe and chimney, three cylinders with divided drive, three sets of Walschaerts gear and the wheelbase extended to 38ft 5in produced a machine in which the Gresley influence had virtually been eliminated.

G

150 and 151. L.N.E. Fifty more Class A1 Pacifics were put into service by the L.N.E.R. in 1923–5. Trouble occurred with the middle valve over running and causing middle big-end failures. This was the Achilles Heel of Gresley's Pacifics until very late in their lives. In 1925 the Locomotive Exchange Trials proved the superiority of the Great Western No. 4079 PENDENNIS CASTLE over Gresley's No. 4474. With some reluctance, Churchward's lessons were learned on the East Coast and all the A1 Pacifics received long travel, long lap valves. They could now be driven with full regulator, well notched up and coal consumption fell from 50 lb to 38 lb per mile. In 1927 No. 4480 ENTERPRISE was rebuilt with a larger superheater and boiler pressure raised from 180 p.s.i. to 220 p.s.i. This was the first Class A3. No. 2544 was similarly rebuilt and the cylinders were reduced from 20in to $18\frac{1}{4}$in diameter. In 1928, twenty-seven new A3's had 19in diameter cylinders and other modifications including a grid-type steam collector in the dome to prevent priming—the so-called "banjo dome". Ultimately all Class A1 were converted to A3 and **Plate 150** shows B.R. No. 60044 MELTON. Various modifications were carried out on the A3 engines, No. 2751 HUMORIST became a guinea pig for experiments with smoke deflection and with double chimney and blast pipe. One A3 and one A1 ran for a time with A.C.F.I. feed water pumps and heaters and further efforts were made to keep the middle big-end from overheating. Corridor tenders, long non-stop runs, high speeds, phenomenal performances were all a part of the daily routine of these magnificent engines.

After the Second War the Gresley Pacifics were in bad shape. Poor coal and indifferent maintenance resulted in steaming troubles and many failures. Once again Swindon came to the rescue in the person of K. J. Cook who in 1956 was C.M.E. at Doncaster. He fitted the A3's (and A4's) with double blast pipes and chimneys, replaced the nickel chrome steel rods with those of normal steel and designed a Great Western type of marine big-end for the middle connecting rod. So in their last years, often with inexperienced firemen and bad coal the A3's gave many of their best performances.

Plate 151 shows B.R. 60071 TRANQUIL as modified.

152. L.N.E. The ultimate development of the East Coast Pacific came in 1935 with H. N. Gresley's Class A4. They were designed primarily for light-weight very-high-speed trains such as the 220-ton *Silver Jubilee* which ran between Newcastle and London in 4 hours. In 1937 the *Coronation* between London and Edinburgh took 6 hours only, including stops at York and Newcastle, and with a 312-ton train of nine special coaches. The A4's on this and on regular non-streamline trains, proved very fast and capable of handling the heaviest East Coast express loadings. The mechanical layout of the engines was the same as that of Class A3 but the cylinders were reduced to $18\frac{1}{2}$in diameter and the piston valves increased to 9in diameter. "Internal streamlining" of all steam passages reflected the work of Chapelon in France. Boiler pressure was 250 p.s.i. A beautiful streamline form was evolved giving a worthwhile saving of horsepower at high speeds as well as being a successful publicity promotion. It also kept the exhaust clear of the cab. In the cab, the men were provided with bucket type seats and Flaman speed indicators were fitted. The A4's rode superbly and at over 100 m.p.h. were comfortable and steady vehicles. Thirty-five were built of which four had Kylchap double chimneys and blast pipes which considerably improved their running at high speeds. Troubles with the middle big-end, resulting from over running of the middle piston valve due to inequalities in the conjugate valve gear, were more marked in the A4's than in other Gresley engines and there were many failures from this cause. As a result of conditions described under **Plate 151,** all the A4's ultimately had double blast pipes and chimneys and modified middle big-ends.

Plate 152. No. 4468 MALLARD as built with Kylchap blast pipe. This locomotive achieved a world speed record for steam of 126 m.p.h. on July 3rd, 1938—and melted all the bearing metal in her middle big-end in doing so.

Plate 153. B.R. No. 60012 COMMONWEALTH OF AUSTRALIA with single blast pipe and chimney. Edward Thompson had the vallances cut away to facilitate maintenance and to enable oiling without the use of flares during the blackout of the 1939/45 War.

154. L.N.E. B.R. 60025 FALCON, Class A4, in its final form working a freight train in to Millerhill Yard, Edinburgh.

Edward Thompson designed his East Coast Pacifics on quite a different plan from Gresley and all of them had three cylinders with divided drive, the inside cylinder driving the leading coupled axle and the outside cylinders the second. Three independent sets of Walschaerts valve gear replaced the Gresley conjugate gear and double blast pipes and chimneys were fitted. Except in the case of the rebuilt GREAT NORTHERN (**Plate 149**) all Thompson's Pacifics had 6ft 2in coupled wheels with a wheelbase about 1ft more than the 35ft 9in of Gresley's Pacifics. The first Thompson Pacifics were a 1943 rebuild of Gresley's six 3-cylinder 2—8—2s of Class P2 (**Plate 156A,** opposite), which were designed for the Edinburgh–Aberdeen road. Their 19ft 6in rigid wheelbase proved too long for the severe curves of the route and they suffered badly from cracked frames. As rebuilt (**Plate 156,** opposite) they were L.N.E. Class A2/2 and were disliked in Scotland as with their lower factor of adhesion they tended to slip badly. The original boilers were retained in the rebuilds with the barrel shortened from 19ft to 17ft.

Thompson's next four Pacifics of Class A2/1 were built in 1944. They were originally ordered as 2—6—2s of Class V2 but were re-designed as Pacifics with a Class B1 bogie, 19in diameter cylinders and steam reversers. The V2 boiler was retained.

Plate 155 (Above). shows No. 509 WAVERLEY, Class A2/1, with an up express passing Berwick. These engines originally had electric lighting and the dynamo, driven from the left hand trailing bogie wheel, can be seen in the picture.

156 (Above). L.N.E. B.R. No. 60503 LORD PRESIDENT, Class A2/2, rebuilt from 2—8—2 Class P2.

156A (right). L.N.E. B.R. No. 2004 MONS MEG Class, P2, as built. The first engine of the class had R. C. Lentz valves and different streamlining.

157 (Below). L.N.E. B.R. No. 60515 SUN STREAM, Class A2/3. This was Thompson's new Pacific design with 6ft 2in wheels. Cylinders were 19in diameter but boiler pressure was raised to 250 p.s.i. The first of the class, No. 500 EDWARD THOMPSON was the 2,000th engine built at Doncaster. Only fifteen of these engines were built and they appeared in 1946 after Thompson's retirement. Originally the design omitted the "banjo dome" but this was reinstated by Peppercorn.

158 and 159. L.N.E. A. H. Peppercorn became C.M.E. of the London and North Eastern Railway in 1946. The original order for Thompson's Class A2/3 (**Plate 157**) was for thirty engines, but only fifteen were built, the second fifteen being re-designed by Peppercorn and introduced in 1947 as Class A2. Many of the features of the Thompson engines were retained—19in cylinders, divided drive, independent valve gear and 6ft 2in coupled wheels. The layout was, however, altered so that the engine wheelbase was shortened by 2ft 7in. The outside cylinders were located further forward between the bogie wheels and a single blast pipe and chimney were fitted. The boiler was made of nickel steel and a Gresley steam collector was incorporated in the dome. To many, these engines were a return to sanity in East Coast Pacific design. No. 525, the first of the class, was the last engine built at Doncaster before nationalisation and was named A. H. PEPPERCORN. Like all the Pacifics with 6ft 2in wheels they were classified as mixed traffic engines and had a high freight power rating.

Plate 158 (Top). B.R. No. 60537 BACHELORS BUTTON, Class A2, leaving King's Cross with a north bound express.

Plate 159 (Lower). B.R. No. 60532 BLUE PETER was one of five Class A2 which were rebuilt with double blast pipes and chimneys and with multiple valve regulators in the superheater header. (No. 60539 was built new with double blast pipe and chimney).

160 and 161. L.N.E. In 1946, after nationalisation, the first of A. H. Peppercorn's express locomotives was introduced. They were classified A1 and the remainder of the original Gresley A1's which had not, by that time, been converted to Class A3, were re-classified A10. The new A1's were identical in layout with the Peppercorn mixed traffic Class A2 and 19in diameter cylinders with 10in piston valves were retained. The boilers with 17ft between tube plates and 250 p.s.i. pressure were interchangeable with those of the A2's. Like all Thompson and Peppercorn engines they had rocking grates and hopper ash-pans; they all had electric lighting from turbo generators and speed recorders were fitted. The main differences were in the provision of 6ft 8in coupled wheels and of double blast pipes and chimneys to all the fifty engines of the class. The original plain-topped chimneys were later given flanged tops which were less severe looking and greatly improved the appearance of the engines. Five engines had roller bearing axleboxes throughout but otherwise no major modifications were applied to any of the class. It is probable that, if in the light of further experience, H. N. Gresley could have been induced to give up his conjugate valve gear and single-axle drive, his later engines could well have followed closely the Peppercorn design. The A1's were excellent engines which ran well and steamed well and they required less maintenance than any other of the major express locomotive types on British Railways, attaining nearly 95,000 miles between general overhauls. The only criticism levelled against them was one of hard and rough riding. Certainly they never rode nearly so well as did the Gresley Pacifics, and much of this could be attributed to the bogie design. One of the A1's was, in fact, fitted with a Gresley swing-link bogie and the improvement in riding was very great. With the end of steam locomotion already in sight, however, no further engines were altered.

Plate 160 (Top). B.R. No. 60156 GREAT CENTRAL, one of the Class A1 with roller bearings, heading a down express north of Potters Bar.

Plate 161 (Lower). B.R. No. 60124 had its name plates (KENILWORTH) and work plates removed to prevent the thieving which became commonplace in Britain towards the end of steam.

162. Southern. B.R. No. 35001 CHANNEL PACKET.
O. V. Bulleid's 3-cylinder *Merchant Navy* Class was introduced in 1941 in the midst of the Second War. Originally described as a mixed traffic engine with 6ft 2in wheels it was classed 8P by British Railways. Thirty engines were built and with their smaller *West Country* sisters (**Plate 164**) constituted the most advanced design ever to run in regular service. Bulleid's valve gear was modified Walschaerts in which the motion to rock the link and to actuate the combining lever was derived from a chain-driven counter shaft. It was completely enclosed in an oil bath between the frames, together with the middle crosshead, connecting rod and crank on the second coupled axle. A steam/hydraulic reverser was provided. The cast steel "double disc" coupled wheels had clasp brakes. The boiler had a welded steel firebox with two thermic syphons and the pressure was 280 p.s.i., later reduced to 250 p.s.i. The butterfly type steam-operated firehole doors were pedal controlled. A multiple-jet blast pipe was fitted, and an air-smoothed casing enclosed boiler and cylinders. In service, leaks from the oil bath caused slipping and occasional fires. Valve events were unreliable partly due to the chain drive and partly to the reverser. In 1956 a start was made to rebuild them all with three sets of valve gear, no oil bath and with the casing removed. The excellent boiler remained unaltered.   **Plate 163** (**Below**). B.R. No. 35026 LAMPORT & HOLT LINE as rebuilt.

164 (Above). **Southern.** B.R. No. 34067 TANGMERE, *Battle of Britain* Class, on an up Kent Coast express near Teynham.

O. V. Bulleid's smaller *West Country* Class was introduced during the Second War in 1945. The mechanical layout was identical with that of the *Merchant Navy* Class but the cylinders, boiler and grate area were smaller and the axle load was in consequence 18¾ tons against 21 tons for the larger engines. Like the *Merchant Navy* engines they had electric lighting throughout—an innovation in British practice. In all, one hundred and ten engines were built, the first seventy being *West Country* Class and the rest with minor modifications being the *Battle of Britain* Class, although eighteen of the latter carried West Country names. They had faults, similar to those of the *Merchant Navy* engines, and many, but not all, were similarly rebuilt before the end of steam. In their original form the Bulleid Pacifics, particularly the smaller engines, were notoriously copious spark throwers and started many lineside fires. It was found that as originally draughted, the introduction of self-cleaning plates, which also acted as spark arresters, prevented adequate steaming. Therefore, in 1962 No. 34064, an unrebuilt *Battle of Britain* was equipped with a Giesl ejector and this cured most of the spark throwing. If steam had continued, no doubt the other unrebuilt engines would have received this device **(Plate 316)**.

Plate 165 (Below). B.R. No. 34037 CLOVELLY, *West Country* Class, as rebuilt. A handsome and successful design.

166 and 167. British Railways. Built under the direction of R. A. Riddles, the *Britannia* Class Pacifics were introduced in 1951 and fifty-five were built. They were Britain's first 2-cylinder Pacifics and the design was excellent. Coupled wheels were 6ft 2in and all axles were carried in roller bearings. A tapered boiler, made of carbon manganese steel, had a maximum diameter of 6ft 5½in and was 17ft between tube plates. The wide firebox had a grate area of 42 sq ft. The dome contained a steam dryer and the regulator was of the multiple valve type on the saturated steam side of the superheater header. The cab and footplate were supported by the boiler, providing an excellent "operating platform" and doing away with the fall plate.

Plate 166 (Top). No. 70009 ALFRED THE GREAT leaving Colchester with an up Norwich express. The *Britannias* made their greatest impact on the old Great Eastern main line and literally revolutionised both times and timekeeping.

Plate 167 (Lower). No. 70004 WILLIAM SHAKESPEARE at Dover. After being exhibited at the Festival of Britain, this engine worked the Golden Arrow service between London and Dover for many years, being allocated to Stewarts Lane solely for that duty. Always immaculately turned out, she was a lovely sight at the head of the Pullman train and became one of the most famous of British Locomotives.

168 and 169. British Railways. The *Clan* Class Pacifics appeared in 1952 and were a smaller and lighter version of the *Britannia* Class. The axle load of 18 tons 17 cwt compared with the $20\frac{1}{4}$ tons of the *Britannias*. The *Clans* had smaller cylinders and the boiler had a maximum diameter of 6ft 1in and a grate area of 36 sq ft, with a pressure of 225 p.s.i. Coupled wheels were 6ft 2in. Ten engines only were built and were intended for service in Scotland, but did most of their work on the Liverpool and Manchester to Glasgow services. As so often happens when the proportions of a good design are altered, the results are far from satisfactory. So it was with the *Clans* which were generally poor and "woolly" machines lacking entirely the "punch" of the *Britannias*. Most drivers preferred the *Patriots* (**Plate 134**) which, in some measure, the *Clans* were built to replace.

Plate 168 (Top). No. 72008 CLAN MACLEOD.

Plate 169 (Lower). No. 72004 CLAN MACDONALD.

170 (Above) and **171** (Below). **British Railways** 3-cylinder 4—6—2 No. 71000 DUKE OF GLOUCESTER.
On page 88 the brief, tragic story of 4—6—2 No. 46202 PRINCESS ANNE was mentioned. The destruction of this engine left a gap in the ranks of the Class 8P which it was decided to fill with another Pacific of completely new design and No. 71000 DUKE OF GLOUCESTER appeared in 1954 as the result. Since she would be allocated to the London Midland Region where the Stanier 4-cylinder Pacifics were doing such excellent work, the psychological wisdom of putting among them one only completely different and untried engine might well be questioned. As it turned out, No. 71000 was always regarded as a black sheep and was never highly regarded by London Midland enginemen. A *Britannia* boiler, but altered to give a grate area of 48·6 sq ft, was provided and there was a double blast pipe and chimney. Three cylinders with divided drive suggested the influence of Doncaster rather than Crewe. Steam distribution was by British Caprotti rotary cam poppet valves and the Swindon Test Report on the engine showed that it used less steam per indicated horse-power-hour than any known design. None the less, the boiler ratios were not quite right (another instance of "fiddling about" with a good design) and certainly the firing methods used for the Stanier Pacifics were not conducive to the good steaming of No. 71000. So, what might have become Britain's most outstanding express locomotive design ended a very brief life with a certain amount of ignominy.

172 and 173. L.M.S. In 1933 and only eighteen months after he became C.M.E. of the London Midland and Scottish Railway, W. A. Stanier's first Pacific No. 6200 THE PRINCESS ROYAL was put into traffic. Four cylinders 16½in × 28in, divided drive, 6ft 6in coupled wheels, 22½-ton axle load, 250 p.s.i. pressure, low temperature superheat, all these were features derived from the Great Western *King* Class. The boiler was entirely different, however, and had 45 sq ft of grate area. Also Stanier provided four sets of valve gear to actuate piston valves of 8in diameter with 7¼in travel and 1¾in lap. After trials with No. 6200 and 6201 the first of these was, in 1935, provided with a new boiler with modified heating surfaces and a 32-element superheater—double the size of that of the original boiler. The improvement was dramatic and later that year ten new engines appeared all with the new boiler. The regulator was in the smokebox and the dome housed top-feed apparatus. In later years the top-feed was located in front of the dome which then contained the regulator valve.

Plate 172 (Top). B.R. No. 46212 DUCHESS OF KENT at work on Shap with the down Mid-day Scot express.

Plate 173 (Lower). L.M.S. No. 6205 PRINCESS VICTORIA with high superheat boiler and top-feed dome. In 1947 this engine was altered to have two sets of outside valve gear and rocking shafts to drive the inside valves. The modified and strengthened motion plate and rocking shafts in front of the outside valves are clearly seen.

4—6—2 7P (later 8P)

174A (Right). L.M.S. No. 6226 DUCHESS OF NORFOLK.

After several high speed runs between London and Glasgow had been made with *The Princess Royal* Class, Stanier introduced his larger and streamlined Pacifics in 1937 to work a high-speed train–the *Coronation Scot*. The first engine, No. 6220 CORONATION put up a world record for steam by travelling at 114 m.p.h. on 29th June, 1937, which was later broken by the L.N.E. MALLARD (**Plate 152**). No. 6229 DUCHESS OF HAMILTON changed name and number with No. 6220 to visit New York Worlds Fair in 1939. Owing to the outbreak of war, she did not return until 1943.

174 (Above). L.M.S. No. 6234 DUCHESS OF ABERCORN was one of five *Coronation* Class built in 1938 without streamlining.

175 (Right). L.M.S. From 1946 onwards, the streamlined casings were removed from the *Coronation* Class. For some time these engines retained the sloping top smokeboxes as shown in this view of No. 6222 QUEEN MARY. Smoke deflectors were fitted and the cut-away running plate at the front end may be compared with that of No. 6234 (**Plate 174**). All of the *Coronation* Class Pacifics, streamlined and non-streamlined were given double blast pipes and chimneys from 1938 onwards; the first to be so treated was No. 6234.

176. L.M.S. B.R. No. 46247 CITY OF LIVERPOOL a de-streamlined *Coronation* Class in its final form.
The *Coronation* Class differed from the first Stanier Pacifics in many ways. The cylinders were $\frac{1}{4}$in greater in diameter and the outside cylinders were placed further forward in the frames which enabled the wheelbase to be reduced 9in to 37ft despite an increase in the driving wheel diameter to 6ft 9in. The piston valve diameter was increased by 1in, to 9in, and the inside valves were driven by rocking shafts behind the cylinders and actuated by the outside valve gear. The boiler diameter was increased to a maximum of 6ft 5$\frac{1}{2}$in but the length of the barrel, 20ft 3$\frac{1}{16}$in was the same as that of *The Princess Royal* Class. The working pressure was retained at 250 p.s.i. The tenders were equipped with steam operated coal pushers, an innovation in British practice. The Stanier Pacifics were built for several years after the retirement of their designer and the engines fell into the following groups: Twenty-four streamlined engines, later de-streamlined, built in 1937–40 and 1943; five non-streamlined engines built in 1938 and four similar in 1944; three non-streamlined engines built in 1946 and having cut-away running plates at the front end as had all the de-streamlined engines with one exception. This was B.R. No. 46242 which was involved in the 1942 accident at Harrow. On rebuilding she was given the original style of curved running plates. Double chimneys and blast pipes and smoke deflectors became standard for all of these fine engines. The final two engines were modified by H. G. Ivatt and the first of them No. 6256 was named SIR WILLIAM A. STANIER, F.R.S. **Plate 177** (Below) shows this engine as B.R. No. 46256. These last two engines had roller bearings throughout and the superheater heating surface was increased to 979 sq ft, a British record! The rear-end framing was re-designed involving changes in the trailing truck. Rocking grates and hopper ashpans were also incorporated in the design.

0—8—0

The world's first 0—8—0 tender locomotive was probably that built for the Baltimore and Ohio Railroad in 1844 to the design of Ross Winan. It had outside cylinders and the drive was to a lay shaft geared to the trailing coupled wheels.

The first European 0—8—0 was designed by an Englishman, John Haswell, who was engineer of the Vienna—Raab Railway. It was named VINDOBONA, had outside cylinders and was built by the Imperial and Royal Austrian State Railway Works for the Semmering Trials in 1851.

The first 0—8—0 locomotives to operate in Britain were built in 1886 for the Swedish and Norwegian Railway but were purchased in 1889 by the Barry Railway. They had outside cylinders and vertical slide valves operated by Stephenson Link Motion. The 0—8—0 design was never as widely used in Britain as in Continental Europe although many of the European engines were of the Prussian State Railway Class G8 of which several thousands were built, all with two outside cylinders.

In Britain, inside cylinder 0—8—0s were built for the Caledonian, Great Northern, Hull and Barnsley, Lancashire and Yorkshire and London and North Western Railways of the old companies, and for the London Midland and Scottish Railway later on. The most noteworthy outside cylinder engines were those of the North Eastern Railway which first appeared in 1901 to the designs of Wilson Worsdell. These engines, of Class T, ultimately forty in number, had piston valves while fifty others, classified T1, had slide valves. All of them had saturated boilers. The further development of the North Eastern 0—8—0 is mentioned below (**Plates 178** and **179**). Between 1902 and 1911 J. G. Robinson put eighty-nine outside cylinder 0—8—0s into service on the Great Central Railway. Most of these engines were superheated before withdrawal and some were rebuilt into tank engines (**Plate 306**).

Multi-cylinder 0—8—0s were rare in Britain and apart from the North Eastern Class T3 (below) they were all compounds. The principal engines were one hundred and eleven 3-cylinder compounds built 1893–1900 to F. W. Webb's designs for the London and North Western Railway. These engines had two high pressure cylinders outside and a single low pressure cylinder 30in in diameter, inside the frames. Webb followed these with one hundred and seventy 4-cylinder compounds built 1901–04. Some of these survived to L.M.S. days and many were rebuilt to 2-cylinder simples. In 1905, George Hughes designed and had built ten 4-cylinder compounds for the Lancashire and Yorkshire Railway, the last 0—8—0 compounds to be built in Britain.

0—8—0   6F8F

178 (Opposite, top). L.N.E. B.R. No. 63407. This was one of one hundred and twenty superheated engines of the North Eastern Railway Class T2 (L.N.E. Class Q6) designed by Vincent Raven and built between 1913 and 1921. The 5ft 6in diameter boilers were interchangeable with those of the 4—6—0s of Class S2 (L.N.E. Class B15). Many were active in the North Eastern Region until the Last Days of Steam.

179 (Opposite, lower). L.N.E. B.R. No. 63463 North Eastern Class T3 (L.N.E. Class Q7) fitted with extra air pump for actuating the air-operated ore-wagon doors on the Tyne Dock–Consett line. Class T3 was Vincent Raven's 3-cylinder design and the only British 3-cylinder simple 0—8—0. Fifteen engines were built, five in 1919 and ten after the Amalgamation, in 1924. The boilers were the same as those of the 3-cylinder 4—6—0s of Class S3 (L.N.E. Class B16). All three cylinders drove the second axle and the piston valves were actuated by three sets of Stephenson Link Motion. The T3's were excellent engines and in 1921 trials between Edinburgh and Perth with one of them pitted against a North British S Class (**Plate 67**) and a Great Western 2—8—0 (**Plate 182**) ended with the honours strongly in favour of the North Eastern engine.

180. L.M.S. No. 9410. When George Whale succeeded F. W. Webb as C.M.E. of the London and North Western Railway, he began converting the 3 and 4-cylinder compound 0—8—0s to 2-cylinder simples with saturated boilers. Later, in 1912, superheaters began to be applied to these engines and thereafter new superheater engines were constructed by Bowen Cooke in 1912 and in 1921. The coupled wheels were 4ft 5½in, the inside valve gear was Joys, and the boilers round-topped, but cylinders and boiler pressure varied with the origins of the engines. The London Midland and Scottish Railway rebuilt most of the engines with superheated Belpaire boilers having a working pressure of 175 p.s.i. and standardised the cylinder size as 20½in × 24in. These engines, of Class G2 were strong and free steaming, gave little trouble and more than two hundred and fifty out of an original four hundred and sixty, were among the Last Steam Locomotives.

181. L.M.S. No. 9589 was one of one hundred and seventy engines designed by Henry Fowler and put into service in 1929–30. The Belpaire boilers (but not the smokebox) were the same as those which George Hughes designed for the North Western Class G2 which these engines were built to replace. The working pressure was increased to 200 p.s.i. Long travel piston valves were driven by inside Walschaerts valve gear and the cylinders were 19½in × 26in instead of 20½in × 24in as in the G2. Derby practice, however, provided them with insufficient bearing surfaces and much too small axle boxes so that, although they were powerful and economical engines on coal and water, they frequently "ran hot" and had failures in the motion. As a result, they were all withdrawn from service long before most of the engines they were built to replace.

In the 2—8—0 type, the eight coupled wheels of the 0—8—0 are retained and there is a leading truck which not only is valuable in providing a pair of guide wheels, but also in taking some of the front-end weight off the leading coupled axle. In point of fact the type was not developed from the 0—8—0 but from the 2—6—0 or Mogul. In 1868 the Master Mechanic of the Lehigh Valley Railroad in the United States rebuilt one of that company's 2—6—0s with a backward extension of the frames and an extra pair of coupled wheels in order to accommodate a new boiler of larger dimensions and with a wide fire box. This locomotive was so successful that subsequently many thousands were built in America and all over the world and the type became numerically by far the largest in the world.

The type name of 2—8—0 is Consolidation and stems from the fact that shortly before the new type was produced, the Lehigh Valley Railroad had been formed by the " consolidation of seven smaller railroads ".

In Europe, the 2—8—0 has been widely used for freight duties but also for mixed traffic and passenger duties, especially in heavily graded areas. Among the most interesting 2—8—0 designs may be mentioned the Italian State Railways Group 745 passenger engines in which the leading radial wheel and the leading coupled wheel are mounted in a separate frame to form a Zara bogie in which the radial wheel has about twice the lateral movement of the coupled wheel. This class had inside cylinders but the piston valves were outside the frames.

The first 2—8—0 locomotive in Britain was put into traffic in 1903 to the designs of G. J. Churchward for the Great Western Railway. This company was also alone in Britain in building a 2—8—0 with 5ft 8in wheels for use on fast freight, mixed traffic and even express passenger trains.

In spite of its proven success in other countries, only five British railways used 2—8—0s before the 1923 Amalgamation. These were the Great Western, Great Central, Great Northern, Somerset and Dorset Joint and the London and North Western. In the case of the last of these, the design was really not new as it consisted of the conversion, from 1905 onwards, of thirty-six of Webb's 4-cylinder compound 0—8—0s to 2—8—0s all of which were scrapped many years before 1955. Another 2—8—0 class which was not among the last steam locomotives was H. N. Gresley's Class O1 of which twenty engines were built between 1913 and 1919. Although very similar in appearance to the later 3-cylinder engines of Class O2, they could always be distinguished by the drive being to the third coupled axle whereas in the Class O2, the outside cylinders drove the second coupled axle.

The great majority of Consolidations the world over had two outside high pressure cylinders but two cylinder compounds were known, as also were those with four cylinders. Three simple cylinders were used in Gresley's O2 design for the Great Northern and subsequently London and North Eastern Railways. A few inside cylinder engines were to be found, notably in Sweden and in Italy as already mentioned.

In both World Wars, the 2—8—0 was the principal type preferred for war service by the armies overseas and for freight haulage at home. In the First War the Robinson 2—8—0 with a 17-ton axle loading was the choice for the Railway Operating Division, and in the Second War Stanier's 2—8—0 with a 16-ton axle load was at first preferred. Next came the " Austerity " engines, said to be based on the Stanier design and in which the maximum axle load was $15\frac{1}{2}$ tons.

During the Second War, no fewer than 1,897 bar-framed 2—8—0s were built in the United States by Alco, Baldwin and Lima to the order of the United States War Department, and a number of these engines were used in Britain. Many are still in service in Europe, especially in the Communist countries. Finally, mention should be made of the 110 engines built by the Vulcan Foundry for U.N.R.R.A. in 1946-47 for service in countries of Eastern Europe. Ten were also built for Luxembourg. Known as the *Liberation* Class they had coupled wheels of 4ft 9in diameter and an axle load of $18\frac{1}{4}$ tons. Although they never ran on the railways in Britain they were noteworthy as the last British designed 2—8—0s for the standard gauge.

182 and 183. Great Western. G. J. Churchward designed and Swindon built, Britain's first 2—8—0 in 1903. They were known as the 2800 Class and one hundred and sixty-seven were built, the last in 1942. Although this was a completely new design, it remained fundamentally unaltered over the years and the major change was superheating which was applied to the class from 1909 onwards. Later engines had cylinders $18\frac{1}{2}$in × 30in and the earlier engines, which had 18in diameter cylinders, had them bored out to this larger size; many were given cylinders with outside steampipes.

Plate 182 (Above). B.R. No. 2872 (built in 1918) working an up freight through Bridgend. This was one of the Churchward engines with inside steam pipes and short cab. The shape of the motion plate will be noted.

Plate 183 (Below). B.R. No. 3802 was one of the later engines built under Collett's direction. A larger side-window cab, modified framing and motion plate and cylinders with outside steam pipes made up the principal differences from the older engines. All the engines had vacuum pumps driven off the right hand cross-head and this can be clearly seen in this view. The 2800's were excellent engines and remained fully capable of dealing with heavy freight on the Western Region of British Railways until the end of steam in that region.

184. Great Western. B.R. No. 4704. The Great Western 4700 Class were the only British examples of a mixed traffic 2—8—0. One was built in 1919 and eight in 1922 to Churchward's designs. They had 5ft 8in coupled wheels and were an enlarged version of the 4300 Class 2—6—0. The first engine was under-boilered and was later provided with a much larger boiler with which the later engines were built new. The 4700's spent much of their time working fast freight trains on the West of England main line and between Paddington and Birkenhead, but they were also regularly used on passenger services at weekends. With the S. & D. J. engines (below) they were the only 2—8—0s in Britain regularly to work on passenger trains.

185. Somerset and Dorset. B.R. No. 53807 on Leeds–Bournemouth express passing Chilcompton. The Somerset and Dorset Joint Railway motive power was a Midland responsibility and most locomotives were of Midland design (**Plate 56**). In 1914, however, it was recognised that more powerful locomotives were needed for the heavily graded Bath–Bournemouth line and six 2—8—0s with 4ft 8½in coupled wheels and 4ft 9in diameter Belpaire boilers were built at Derby. In 1925 five more, with 5ft 3in boilers came from Robert Stephenson & Co. Later, these engines received 4ft 9in boilers and No. 53807 was one of these. Two engines were successfully fitted with Ferodo brake blocks. All the S. & D. 2—8—0s suffered from short travel piston valves and inadequate axle boxes.

186. L.N.E. No. 6238 Class O4 working a down freight train near Retford.

J. G. Robinson's 2—8—0 for the Great Central Railway appeared in 1911 as Class 8K (L.N.E. Class O4) and one hundred and thirty were built. They were graceful but strongly built engines which soon became firm favourites with the men. The first engines had Schmidt superheaters but these were soon replaced with those of Robinson's own excellent design. During the First War, the design was chosen for the R.O.D. and five hundred and twenty-one engines were constructed by contractors and at Gorton. Most of these engines had steel fireboxes but were otherwise identical with the Great Central engines. They are perhaps the best known of all British locomotives for they went all over the world and some are still (1966) at work in China and in Australia. With their equal coupled axle loading of only 16½ tons they had a wide route availability. After the War some of the R.O.D. engines went into service on other railways in Britain, notably the Great Western, London and North Western and South Eastern and Chatham, while in 1924 the London and North Eastern bought, very cheaply, two hundred and seventy-three, many of which were new engines but all of which had steel fireboxes. Some of these were sent overseas again in the Second War and did not return home. In 1918, eighteen new engines were built at Gorton with 6ft diameter boilers and some with double window cabs. These were Class 8M (L.N.E. Class O5) and known as the "Tiny's". They later received 5ft boilers and became L.N.E. Class O4. H. N. Gresley gave the engines his hideous "flower-pot" chimneys, and many were provided with a variety of boilers. Some of these are shown opposite. From 1944 onwards, fifty-eight were completely reconstructed with new cylinders 20in × 26in, Walschaerts valve gear and Edward Thompson's 100A boiler with 225 p.s.i. pressure. These engines were Class O1 and **Plate 187** (**below**) shows B.R. No. 63856 fitted with air pumps for operating the doors of the Consett iron-ore wagons.

188. L.N.E. B.R. No. 6242 (ex G.C.R. Class 8K) Class O4/5 with Gresley round-top boiler and separate smokebox saddle, but retaining original cab.

189. L.N.E. B.R. No. 63634 (ex R.O.D.) Class O4/7 with Gresley round-top boiler, but retaining original smokebox and cab.

190. L.N.E. B.R. No. 3828 (ex R.O.D.) Class O4/8 with Thompson 100A boiler and smokebox and double window cab, but retaining original cylinders (21 in × 26 in) and frames.

191. Great Western. B.R. No. 3048 was one of the Robinson-R.O.D. engines bought by the Great Western Railway and fitted with their chimney, safety valves and top feed.

192. L.N.E. B.R. No. 2437, Class O2/3, was one of the last batch of H.N. Gresley's 3-cylinder freight engines introduced with No. 461 (later Class O2/1) in 1918. This engine had inclined cylinders and Gresley's conjugated valve gear in its original form. At Holcroft's suggestion all the other engines had level cylinders and the conjugated levers in front of the steam chests. Class O2/2 had Great Northern type cabs and smaller tenders than O2/3. They were fine engines, and owing to their normally slow operating speeds, suffered much less from middle big-end troubles than the other Gresley 3-cylinder machines.

193. L.M.S. B.R. No. 48500 on a coal train near Halton. W. A. Stanier's 2—8—0 was introduced in 1935. Two outside cylinders, Walschaerts valve gear and a taper boiler were features of these very successful engines which had an axle load of only 16 tons. The first engines had low temperature superheaters and regulators in the smokeboxes, but later (and ultimately all) engines had domed boilers, larger grates, and larger superheaters. One hundred and twenty-six were built for the L.M.S. before the War, but the design was adopted by the Ministry of Supply and a further two hundred and forty were built, most of which, together with some of the L.M.S. engines, went to Egypt, Iran, Turkey and other Middle East countries. Also during the War, large numbers were built at the Locomotive Works of the three other railways for service all over Britain ; more than six hundred and fifty were among the Last Steam Locomotives.

194. B.R. No. 90062 on an up coal train south of Peterborough. The Ministry of Supply "Austerity" 2—8—0s were designed by R. A. Riddles during the Second War and nine hundred and thirty-four were built between 1943 and 1945. Although Stanier's 2—8—0 was the basis of the design, the engines had round-top boilers similar to those of the L.N.E. engines, cylinders 19in × 28in, and the metallurgy reflected the need for economy in high grade ferrous and non-ferrous metals. Many saw service in France, Holland and Belgium but most returned to Britain after the War and British Railways had seven hundred and thirty-three of them in 1955.

195. No. 2290 after it had been fitted with an electric headlight, the power for which was obtained from a small turbo-generator which can be seen located under the left hand side of the footplate.

Although ten-coupled engines had been in common use on the Continent for some years, the only example in Britain had been a short-lived 3-cylinder 0—10—0 well-tank engine designed by J. Holden for the Great Eastern Railway in 1902. Then, in 1919, that traditional birthplace of small engines Derby Midland Railway Works, produced Britain's second ten-coupled engine, a massive 4-cylinder machine for banking trains up the three miles at 1 in 37 of the Lickey Incline. Only one engine, No. 2290, was ever built and it remained the only British example of the 0—10—0 tender engine and the only ten-coupled engine until 1943 (**Plate 196**). The four cylinders, $16\frac{3}{4}$in $\times$ 28in, were inclined at 1 in 7 and each pair (inside and outside cylinders of each side) had crossed ports and a common outside-admission piston valve 10in in diameter. This was the first and only British example of this practice and owing to space limitation the piston valve had to be located above the outside cylinder of each pair, instead of equidistantly above and between them as in Continental practice. The piston valves were driven by two sets of outside Walschaerts gear. All of the 4ft $7\frac{1}{2}$in coupled wheels were flanged and the drive from all four cylinders was to the middle pair. The parallel boiler was 5ft 3in in diameter and the grate area 31.5 sq ft. Four Ramsbottom safety valves were provided. The tender, which had a tender cab, was that which ran behind the Paget experimental 2—6—2 (Page 41). "Big Bertha" or "Big Emma" as she was variously called, worked 36 years before being withdrawn in 1956. A spare boiler was kept at Derby for the engine so that the time out of service for repairs was reduced to a minimum.

2—10—0 8F

The first 2—10—0 or Decapod type was, like the first 2—8—0, designed and built for the Lehigh Valley Railroad. In 1869 that Company's enterprising Master Mechanic added a fifth pair of coupled wheels to two 2—8—0s to produce two 2—10—0s named BEE and ANT.

The type was widely used in Europe, notably in Austria, France, Germany and Italy many years before it came to Britain, outstanding designs being those of the Austrian Southern Railway and those of the Prussian State Railways from which the French Eastern Railway 3-cylinder engines were copied. Later German State Railways designs were built in very large numbers before and during the Second War and included the Series 52 Kriegsloks, which were to be found in nearly every European country and many still remain.

European 2—10—0s were used for heavy freight haulage, but also were frequently found at the head of passenger trains and most of them had a maximum speed of 50 m.p.h. In Greece, 2—10—0s of Austrian design were for many years the principal express engines.

The first British 2—10—0s were, like their American forbears, enlargements of an existing 2—8—0 design. They were designed by R. A. Riddles as " Austerity " engines in 1943 and one hundred and fifty were built during the next two years by the North British Locomotive Company. Most of them were sent to Holland and Belgium but a few went to the Middle East. Twenty-five came into British Railways stock.

There were several interesting points about the design, mainly in the boiler which had a wide firebox and a rocking grate with 40 sq ft of grate area. The inner firebox was of steel and had three arch tubes. The middle pair of coupled wheels were without flanges, the coupled wheel diameter was 4ft 8½in, the same as for the 2—8—0s, and there was the same economical use of materials.

The only other British 2—10—0 was the Class 9 built for British Railways and described in the next pages.

196. B.R. No. 90774 NORTH BRITISH, one of the "Austerity" 2—10—0s described above is here seen working an up freight and descending Beattock incline.

197 (Above). B.R. No. 92063 with single blast-pipe and chimney. The British Railways Class 9F engines were designed under the direction of R. A. Riddles and first went into service in 1954. They were an immediate success and two hundred and fifty-one were built—the last in 1960 being the last steam locomotive to be built for British Railways. The boiler, of a new design, had the regulator in the dome but operated by outside rodding which entered the boiler through a stuffing box. Rocking grate, hopper ashpan and self-cleaning smokebox were fitted and the cab and footplate were supported by the boiler. The axle load was only 15½ tons and the middle pair of coupled wheels were flangeless. With a coupled wheel diameter of 5ft these engines were often employed on passenger train duties, and unlike most of the Continental 2—10—0s, were not limited to 50 m.p.h. In fact 90 m.p.h. was recorded on at least one occasion and 60–70 m.p.h. in both passenger and fast freight service was commonplace. Berkley mechanical stokers were fitted to three engines of which **Plate 198 (below)** shows No. 92166. As they were put to work on poor coal and dust, the stokers, which were designed to use graded coal, were not successful. Furthermore, the Americans proved that stokers were not economical in use with less than 50 sq ft of grate area, and the 9F's had grates of only 40·2 sq ft.

199. B.R. No. 92029 with Crosti boiler. In 1955, ten locomotives of Class 9F were built with Crosti boilers having single preheaters. This, and the Franco-Crosti boiler, with two pre-heaters, were claimed to have made great savings in coal on Italian locomotives (a reduction of 17½ per cent was claimed at one large F.S. depot). The best that could be claimed for the Crosti 9F was of the order of 2 to 4 per cent and the disadvantages far outweighed this small economy. The flow of hot gasses from the fire was slowed up and cooled by the pre-heater being in circuit. This allowed the formation of sulphuric acid which seriously corroded the tubes and tube plates of the pre-heater and also the chimneys. Trouble was experienced even with corrosion of the superheater elements. The location of the chimney in front of the right hand side of the cab, made the Crosti engines dirty and objectionable to work, and no-one regretted the removal of the pre-heaters, even though as "normal" engines the smaller diameter boiler was retained.

200. B.R. No. 92250 with Giesl ejector.
With a single blast pipe and chimney the Class 9F boiler could produce 27,000 lb of steam per hour—adequate for most duties. By fitting a well-designed double blast pipe and chimney the maximum output of the boiler was raised to 30,000 lb per hour and from 1957 many engines were so fitted (**Plate 198**). In order to try to reduce coal consumption, a Giesl ejector was fitted to No. 92250 and exhaustive trials carried out at Rugby test plant under the supervision of Dr. Giesl—Gieslingen himself. A saving in coal of from 4 to 5 per cent was achieved using good quality coal, but this was insufficient inducement to warrant the equipping of further locomotives with the ejector.

Experimental 4—6—4 8P7F

201A (Right). L.N.E. H. N. Gresley's 4-cylinder compound high pressure locomotive No. 10000, Class W1 appeared in 1929. It had a 5-drum watertube Yarrow boiler with 450 p.s.i. pressure and 35 sq. ft. of grate. H.P. cylinders were inside the frames and L.P. outside. Two sets of Walschaerts gear outside drove the 8in L.P. piston valves and the 6in H.P. valves through rocking shafts which had slotted inside arms fitted with die blocks connected to the inside combination levers. Thus was independent cut-off for H.P. and L.P. valves made possible. The boiler was unsatisfactory, largely because it was impossible to prevent air leaks which resulted in poor steaming. In 1937, No. 10000 was reconstructed with three 20in × 26in cylinders, Gresley-Walschaerts valve gear and a conventional boiler with 250 p.s.i. pressure and 50 sq ft grate area. The Cartazzi radial wheels and the Bissel truck at the rear end, were retained. **Plate 201** (centre) shows the rebuilt engine and **Plate 202** (lower) as B.R. No. 60700 with vallances removed by Thompson.

TANK LOCOMOTIVES

A tank locomotive may be defined as a locomotive engine which carries supplies of coal and water on its own chassis and not in a separate vehicle or tender. The French, being essentially logical, refer to such engines as "locomotives–tenders" as distinct from "locomotives a tender séparé" which is what *we* call tender locomotives.

The origin of the tank locomotive is uncertain. In Warren's *A Century of Locomotive Building* there is reference to a letter of 16th January, 1828, written by John B. Jervis, Chief Engineer of the Delaware and Hudson Canal Company (of America): "It is desirable to dispense with the tender carriage, to have a water tank fixed to the engine carriage . . .". Whether any such engine was built at that time is uncertain and the first firm knowledge of a tank locomotive's being built is (according to Ahrons) one constructed by Dr. Church of Birmingham in 1837. About the same time two four-wheeled tank engines were constructed by Forrester and Co. for the Dublin and Kingstown Railway.

As the great cities grew and railways increasingly extended their role in suburban transportation, so the tank engine became more and more important, with its ability to run in either direction with equal facility and its economy of space when compared with a tender engine. Its convenience in working branch lines and indeed in any areas where turntable facilities were not easily available made it an attractive proposition to railway operators. For work in docks and the restricted areas of factory sidings it became indispensible and for all forms of shunting and hump operation the tank engine ruled supreme.

Tank locomotives fall into four main groups:

(1) those in which the water is carried in two *side tanks* and usually also in a third tank below the coal bunker.

(2) those in which the water is carried in a *well tank* between the frames. This form of engine has never found favour in Britain but is widely used in Continental Europe often in conjunction with side tanks which can then be made smaller.

(3) those in which the water is carried in a *saddle tank* on top of the boiler. Long saddle tanks extend over the whole length of boiler and smokebox; short saddles do not cover the smokebox and in some cases, only part of the boiler.

(4) *pannier tanks* are slung on each side of the boiler and are a modification of the saddle tank; they were introduced by the Great Western Railway to permit the use of a Belpaire boiler. A saddle tank over a square-topped Belpaire firebox would be very difficult to manufacture and to maintain. Pannier tanks may be "long" or "short" as may saddle tanks.

The advantages gained from saddle and pannier tanks are mainly those which stem from the ease of access afforded to cranks, motion, etc., between the frames. Their disadvantages are in the limited tank capacity and the fact that so large a weight placed high up on the engine raises problems of stability and no engines designed for high speeds have ever had such tanks.

One of the principal disadvantages of all tank engines lies in the fact that, as the journey or duty progresses and the water is used up, so the weight available for adhesion becomes progressively less and bad slipping may arise from this cause.

While many tank engines have been involved in regular operation of express train services the largest express tank engines, the Baltic or 4—6—4 type were never successful. The London Tilbury and Southend, the London Brighton and South Coast, the Lancashire and Yorkshire, and the Glasgow and South Western all had fine-looking outside cylinder 4—6—4 tanks, the L. & Y. engines having four cylinders. The double-ended design always raised the problem of stability at high speeds due to the movement, despite baffles, of the large volume of water in the side tanks. Probably the L. B. & S. C. were the most successful and they carried much of their water in a well tank between the frames. The Furness introduced some non-superheater inside cylinder 4—6—4 tanks which, in view of the geography of their route were never required to run very fast.

It was left to the modern 2—6—2 and 2—6—4 tank engines to demonstrate that high speeds could be safely attained by engines having efficient bogie and radial wheel control. In the common 0—6—2 wheel arrangement the trailing axle was mounted in radial axle boxes where stability was more important than flexibility, but where greater flexibility was needed then the trailing axle was in a radial or Bissel truck.

The number of tank engines used on British railways has always been substantial and the variety of tank engine types exceeded that of tender engines. The Great Western Railway had the highest proportion of tank engines to tender engines of all the four railways before nationalisation. At the commencement of the period covered by this book, nearly 64 per cent of the locomotive stock of the Western Region was composed of tank engines. At the same time the proportion of tank engines in the whole of British Railways stock was about 35 per cent.

0—4—0T 0F 3F 0F 0—4—0ST 0F

203. L.N.E. B.R. No. 68126. Great Eastern Railway Class B77. L.N.E. Class Y4. A. J. Hill had five of these squat little dock tanks built between 1913 and 1921. They had Belpaire boilers, Walschaerts valve gear and, as built, the chimneys were much taller.

204. Great Western. B.R. No. 1103. In 1926 the G.W.R. purchased six powerful dock shunting engines from the Avonside Engine Co. They had domed Belpaire boilers, Walschaerts valve gear and the cabs were modified to the shape shown after 1931. A warning bell was fixed in front of the spectacle plate during the Second War.

205. L.M.S. No. 1534 was one of R. M. Deeley's ten shunting tank engines for works and collieries sidings. They had Walschaerts valve gear and round-topped boilers. They were built to replace Johnson's 1883 inside cylinder 0—4—0 Saddle Tanks, but a few of these little engines lasted into the Last Days of Steam.

206. L.M.S. No. 11234. This was one of fifty-seven Lancashire and Yorkshire Saddle Tanks built in batches between 1891 and 1910 to the designs of J. A. F. Aspinall. They had Stephenson's Link Motion inside the frames and the saddle tanks ran the length of the boiler and smokebox. The safety valves were inside the cab and had extension tubes fitted to carry the steam through the cab roof. Coal was carried inside the side sheets of the cab.

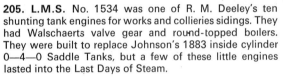

207. L.N.E. B.R. No. 68102. North British Railway Class G. L.N.E. Class Y9. Built between 1882 and 1899 these popular little "Pugs" were designed by M. Holmes. They usually trailed behind them wooden-bodied 4-wheeled tenders which were converted from ancient wagons. Thirty-five were built and they were a familiar sight in the docks of the East Coast of Scotland.

208. L.M.S. B.R. No. 56020. Photographed in Derby Shed, this Caledonian "Pug" was far from home and without its familiar wooden-bodied 4-wheeled tender. Pop safety valves and stove pipe chimney were also later additions. Fourteen engines were built between 1895 and 1908 under the direction of J. F. McIntosh to a previous Drummond design.

209. Great Western. B.R. No. 1140 was built in 1905 for the Swansea Harbour Trust by Andrew Barclay & Co. After the 1923 Amalgamation it was given a G.W. safety-valve casing and other modifications including a warning bell in front of the cab, and better shelter was provided for the enginemen.

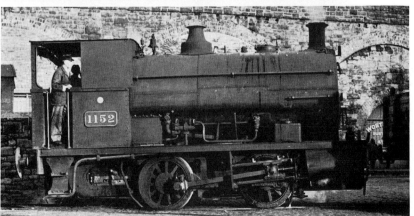

210. Great Western. B.R. No. 1152. This was one of three Peckett tanks taken over by the Great Western Railway in 1923 from Messrs. Powlesand and Mason of Swansea. The G.W. safety valve cover and the warning bell will be noted. It was employed shunting in Swansea Docks.

211. B.R. No. 47007. Five 0—4—0ST were built by Kitson and Co. in 1932 to W. A. Stanier's design. These engines had 800-gallon saddle tanks and bunker space for 1 ton of coal. In 1953 a further five engines were built at Horwich of which No. 47007 was one. These engines had shorter but deeper saddle tanks to carry 800 gallons of water but the bunker space was extended to carry 2 tons of coal. Other dimensions were identical with the L.M.S. engines.

212 (right). Southern. B.R. No. 30589. This was one of ten engines of L.S.W. Class C14 designed by Dugald Drummond and built in 1906 as 2—2—0T for motor-train working. Six were sold to the Government during the First War and the others were converted to 0—4—0T in which state two were shunting at Southampton Docks for many years.

213 (below). Southern. B.R. No. 30084, Class B4 (Drummond 1908) working a transfer freight from the Eastern to the Western Docks at Dover. W. Adams introduced his dock-shunting engine in 1891 for the London and South Western Railway, and twenty were built. In 1908, Dugald Drummond built five further engines, with "lock up" safety valves on the dome and they were Class K14. Later, all the engines were Classed B4; fourteen carried names and these were used for shunting at Southampton Docks before the arrival of the U.S.A. tanks (**Plate 267**).

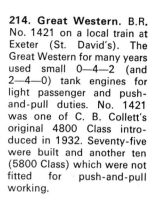

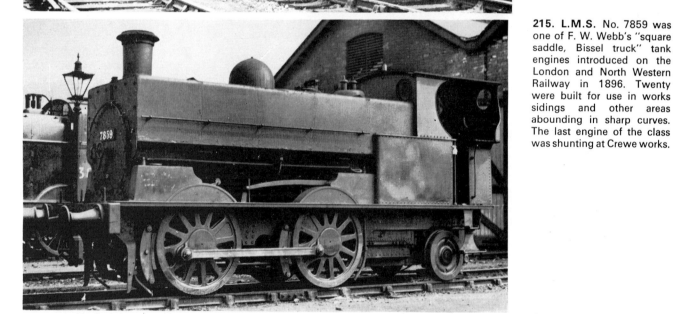

214. Great Western. B.R. No. 1421 on a local train at Exeter (St. David's). The Great Western for many years used small 0—4—2 (and 2—4—0) tank engines for light passenger and push-and-pull duties. No. 1421 was one of C. B. Collett's original 4800 Class introduced in 1932. Seventy-five were built and another ten (5800 Class) which were not fitted for push-and-pull working.

215. L.M.S. No. 7859 was one of F. W. Webb's "square saddle, Bissel truck" tank engines introduced on the London and North Western Railway in 1896. Twenty were built for use in works sidings and other areas abounding in sharp curves. The last engine of the class was shunting at Crewe works.

216. L.N.E. No. 6832, Great North of Scotland Class Y, L.N.E. Class Z5, was one of two 0—4—2T, with 4ft coupled wheels and 14in × 20in cylinders, built by Manning Wardle & Co. in 1915 to the designs of T. E. Heywood for service in Aberdeen Docks. Another two similar engines were built during the same year, but had 3ft 6in coupled wheels and the cylinders were 13in × 20in.

217. Southern. B.R. No. 30586. The last 2—4—0 tank engines of British Railways were three Class 0298 of the old London and South Western Railway. They were well-tanks supplied by Beyer Peacock & Co in 1875 to the designs of W. G. Beattie, and were the survivors of a once numerous class used on the London suburban services. They had inside Allan Link Motion and many, in their early days, had feed-water pumps worked off the cross-heads. The engines were rebuilt at least three times during their long lives and No. 30586 is seen with a Drummond boiler and chimney but retaining the rectangular splashers with which the later engines were fitted. The reason for their longevity was their 12½-ton axle load and 12ft 6in wheelbase which were both well suited to the lightly laid branch lines which serve the China Clay deposits at Wenford Bridge and Ruthern Bridge, near Wadebridge in Cornwall.

218. Southern. B.R. No. W26 WHITWELL on a Ryde to Ventnor train. Class O2 of the London and South Western Railway consisted of sixty engines built between 1889 and 1895 to the designs of W. Adams. They replaced the Beattie 2—4—0 well-tanks on many branch line duties. The last survivors of the Class were from the twenty-one which worked in the Isle of Wight and had enlarged bunkers and Westing-house pumps. Some had Drummond boilers and all the Island engines were named.

219. Southern. No. 130 was one of Dugald Drummond's 0—4—4T for the London and South Western Railway and a familiar sight at Waterloo where for years many were station pilots. The first fifty-five engines built 1897–1900 were Class M7; the fifty engines built 1903-11, with minor modifications such as slightly longer frames, were Class X14 and No. 130 was one of these. All were later classed M7. No. 126 ran for some years with a super-heater boiler as fitted to the rebuilt 700 Class 0—6—0 **(Plate 54)**.

220. L.M.S. No. 15053 was Highland Railway Class W, one of four engines designed by Peter Drummond and built in 1905. This engine worked the Dornoch Branch for many years and was the last Highland engine in service on British Railways.

221. L.M.S. B.R. No. 58071 with round top boiler and condensing gear, was one of S. W. Johnson's second series of 0—4—4T for the Midland Railway. One hundred and sixty-five engines were built between 1881 and 1900 and many were rebuilt with Belpaire boilers and pop safety valves. There were variations in cylinder diameter and working pressure but all had 5ft 4in coupled wheels compared with the earlier (1875) engines which had 5ft 7in coupled wheels.

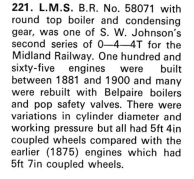

222. L.M.S. No. 6408. Although attributed to W. A. Stanier and appearing in 1932, ten 0—4—4T were a modernised version of the Midland Johnson 0—4—4T with larger cylinders. The stove pipe chimney was a surprise to Stanier as it was to all railwayists and stemmed from the fact that all of Stanier's original outline drawings were shown with stovepipes, as the chimney shape for future L.M.S. engines had not then been decided. The ten 0—4—4T later had Stanier chimneys.

223. L.M.S. B.R. No. 55208. J. F. McIntosh introduced his 5ft 9in passenger tank engines in 1895 and one hundred were built during the next twenty years. The main difference between earlier and later engines was increased tank and bunker capacity, No. 55208 being one of the later engines with 2½ ton bunkers and 1,270 gallon tanks. The stove pipe chimney was introduced after the Second War. Pickersgill built more of these useful engines with small modifications, and the L.M.S. constructed a further ten in 1925. They were used on Glasgow Suburban duties, on many branch lines, and some had strengthened buffer beams for banking up Beattock.

224. L.N.E. B.R. No. 67337 was North Eastern Railway Class O, L.N.E. Class G5, designed by Wilson Worsdell and introduced in 1894. This was one of eighteen of the class which were fitted for push-and-pull working. One hundred and ten of these tough little engines were built and they did a lot of very hard work on the North East Coast. In the late nineteen thirties they worked the Seven Sisters—Palace Gates service.

225. Southern. B.R. No. 31544 was South Eastern and Chatham Class H designed by H. S. Wainwright and introduced in 1904. Sixty-six engines were scheduled but only sixty-four were built until Maunsell discovered the error in 1915 and the last two engines appeared, six years late. British Railways equipped forty-four, including No. 31544, for push-and-pull working.

226. L.M.S. No. 10713 Lancashire and Yorkshire Railway Class 5 with short bunker was one of J. A. F. Aspinall's 2—4—2T with Joy's valve gear which went into service in 1889. Three hundred and thirty were built up to the end of 1911, and they ably handled much express passenger traffic. They had water scoops for both forward and backward running. H. A. Hoy and George Hughes developed the design which was the subject of many trials and experiments. There were three major design changes: (i) After 1898 the bunkers were enlarged to carry $3\frac{1}{2}$ instead of 2 tons of coal and an extra 200 gallons of water. (ii) From 1902 to 1910 new engines had saturated Belpaire boilers with increased water space and extended smoke boxes, and many earlier engines were so rebuilt. **Plate 227** (centre) shows L.M.S. No. 10693 with short bunker as rebuilt. (iii) In 1911, twenty engines were built with Belpaire superheater boilers and some older engines were rebuilt with these boilers. Superheater engines were Class 5 and none survived to be among the Last Steam Locomotives.

228 (below). L.N.E. The Great Eastern Railway owned two hundred and thirty-five 2—4—2 tank engines and used them on branch lines and on London suburban services. B.R. No. 67227 was G.E. Class G69, L.N.E. Class F6 designed by S. D. Holden in 1911 (see also **Plate 229**).

229. L.N.E. B.R. No. 67200 on a push-and-pull train at Ongar. Great Eastern Class M15R, L.N.E. Class F5, consisted of thirty engines of Class M15 (L.N.E. F4) built 1903–9 by J. Holden and rebuilt with 180 p.s.i. boilers by S. D. Holden in 1911–20. They had Stephenson Link Motion and were similar in power to Class F6 (**Plate 228**) but had smaller tanks and did not have side-window cabs. They were employed on similar duties.

230. Southern. No. 3488 working a train from Axminster to Lyme Regis. The London and South Western 415 Class were built between 1882 and 1885 and consisted of seventy-one engines designed by W. Adams. All were scrapped or disposed of in the nineteen-twenties except two which were kept for working the Lyme Regis branch. A third engine, No. 3488, was bought back from the East Kent Railway in 1946.

231 (below). L.M.S. B.R. No. 41946 on up express at Shoeburyness. Thirty-five non-superheater 4—4—2T were built 1923–30 for the Tilbury lines of the L.M.S. They were replacements of earlier No. 1 Class engines and were almost identical with the L. T. & S. 79 Class but had extended smokeboxes.

232. L.N.E. No. 7368 on a train from Essendine near Stamford. In 1898, H. A. Ivatt put into service on the Great Northern Railway, ten 4—4—2T with 5ft 8in wheels for working the London Suburban services. They were fitted with condensing apparatus and a further fifty were built during the next nine years. They became L.N.E. Class C12 and were never superheated, the boiler being interchangeable with L.N.E. Class J4 0—6—0. When the more powerful 0—6—2T were built, the 4—4—2T were displaced from the London area, their condensing gear was removed and they worked on various branch lines for many years. The later engines of the series had wider bunker tops which can be seen in this view of No. 7368.

233. L.N.E. B.R. No. 67474 on push-and-pull train for Arrochar at Helensburgh. W. P. Reid designed these sturdy little tank engines for the North British Railway and thirty were built between 1911 and 1913. They were not super-heated and had slide valves. On the North British they were Class M and on the L.N.E. Class C15.

234. L.N.E. No. 9452 on an Edinburgh suburban train passing Craigentinny. The North British Class L, L.N.E. Class C16 was W. P. Reid's superheated tank engine of 1915–21. Twenty-one were built and they had 1in. larger diameter cylinders than the preceding class. Piston valves above the cylinders resulted in a higher-pitched boiler but the working pressure was only 165 p.s.i. compared with 175 p.s.i. of the saturated engines.

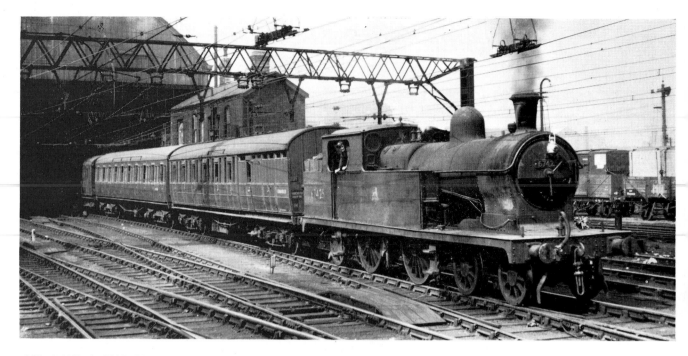

235. L.N.E. In 1903–05, J. G. Robinson put into service on the Great Central Railway, forty non-superheater 4—4—2T for the London Marylebone Suburban services. Like their contemporaries, the Great Northern 4—4—2T (**Plate 232**) working from King's Cross, the Great Central engines were later displaced from the London area by more powerful engines—in this case, 4—6—2T. Some spent most of their lives thereafter, on country branch lines and on such duties as the South Yorkshire Joint line services between Doncaster and Worksop. Most were used for local and suburban services around the great provincial cities Manchester, Liverpool, Sheffield and Nottingham. These engines were Great Central Class 9K, L.N.E. Class C13. Their bunkers carried 3½ tons of coal and their tanks 1,450 gallons of water. They were superheated, most during L.N.E. days, and at which time their elegant appearance was ruined by H. N. Gresley's tapered "flower pot" chimneys. **Plate 235** shows B.R. No. 67425 leaving Manchester (London Road) with a train for Marple.

236. L.N.E. No. 6129 Great Central Class 9L, L.N.E. Class C14. In 1907 a further twelve 4—4—2T were built at Gorton. They were similar to the preceding class but the coal capacity was increased to 4½ tons and they carried 1,825 gallons of water. They were later superheated and had Gresley chimneys, as shown here.

237. Southern. No. 268, Class G6. W. Adams introduced in 1894 this 0—6—0T version of his Class O2 0—4—4T (**Plate 218**), cylinders, boilers and coupled wheels having the same dimensions. Twenty were built and Dugald Drummond added ten more, using Adams boilers intended for the Beattie 2—4—0WT. These ten engines were at first classified M9. Later, some engines received Drummond boilers with safety valves on the dome.

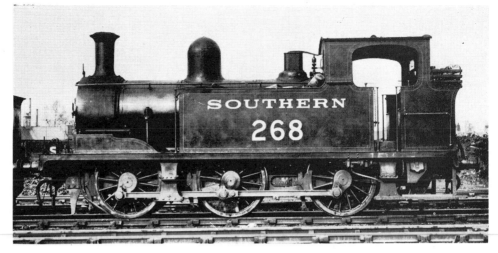

238. Southern. B.R. No. 32644 was one of W. Stroudley's "Terrier" tank engines, fifty of which were built by the London, Brighton and South Coast Railway between 1872 and 1880. They worked originally in the London Suburban area but in their later years were widely scattered. As built they were Class A1 but after being rebuilt with improved boilers and circular smokeboxes by D. E. Marsh and L. B. Billinton (1911–22) the survivors became Class A1X.

239. Southern. B.R. No.31323 Class P. H. S. Wainwright designed these little engines for the South Eastern and Chatham Railway and eight were built at Ashford in 1909–10. They were intended for push-and-pull working and they often worked with two or four coaches, the engine being in the middle. In their later days they were used in the docks at Dover and as shunting engines at various locomotive sheds and sidings.

240. L.N.E. B.R. No. 68577, L.N.E. Class J69/1. This class consisted of new engines of Great Eastern Class S56 and rebuilt engines of Class R24. They were designed by J. Holden and were introduced in 1902, ultimately becoming the most numerous of the many Great Eastern 0—6—0T, 275 of which were at work at the 1923 Amalgamation. They carried $2\frac{1}{2}$ tons of coal and 1,200 gallons of water; their working pressure was 180 p.s.i. and grate area $14\frac{1}{2}$ sq ft. Besides their shunting duties they were, at one time, regularly employed on Liverpool Street Suburban services.

241. L.N.E. B.R. No. 68736, L.N.E. Class J72, specially painted in North Eastern green and carrying the crest of the North Eastern Railway, for passenger shunting duties at York. In 1886, T. W. Worsdell introduced his Class E 0—6—0 tank engine (L.N.E. Class J71) with 4ft $7\frac{1}{4}$in wheels. Many of the 120 built were used for passenger shunting and some survived until 1961. In 1898, W. Worsdell introduced Class E1 (L.N.E. Class J72) similar to Class E but with 4ft $1\frac{1}{4}$in wheels. Eighty-five were built, the last in 1925 and then, in 1949–51, British Railways built a further twenty-eight—a unique building record for an unaltered design.

242. L.N.E. No. 1000 D North Eastern Class 290, L.N.E. Class J77. Between 1874 and 1883, one hundred and thirty 0—4—4WT Class B.T.P. (Bogie Tank Passenger) were built to the designs of E. Fletcher (**Plate 242A,** page 171). Between 1899 and 1904 some of these engines were rebuilt at York as 0—6—0T with round-topped cabs as shown; in 1907 and 1921 further engines were similarly rebuilt at Darlington but these had square cabs. In all, sixty 0—4—4WT were rebuilt to 0—6—0T.

243. L.M.S. No. 1669 was one of two hundred and eighty engines built between 1878 and 1899 for the Midland Railway to the designs of S. W. Johnson. They were a familiar sight on that railway and its derivatives for over ninety years. They carried $1\frac{1}{2}$ tons of coal and the side tanks (only) 740 gallons of water. Working pressure, with round-top boilers, was 140 p.s.i. but from 1924, one hundred and twenty-two were rebuilt with Belpaire boilers with pop safety valves and 150 p.s.i. pressure. Some engines had half-cabs, even when rebuilt while others of both round-top and Belpaire varieties had complete cabs as had No. 1669.

244. Southern. B.R. No. 31069, Class R1 with Stirling type cab, domed boiler and extra sand boxes in front of the leading wheels for working on the 1 in 30 incline between Folkestone Harbour and Folkestone Junction. Between 1888 and 1898, James Stirling put into service twenty-five domeless 0—6—0T of Class R built at the South Eastern Railway Works at Ashford. Working pressure was 140 p.s.i. and they had round-topped cabs. Some had short chimneys for duty on the Canterbury and Whitstable line. From 1902 Wainwright began rebuilding them with 160 p.s.i. domed boilers, and, except for the Whitstable engines, "pagoda" type cabs. These rebuilds were Class R1 and ultimately the whole class was dealt with.

245. Southern. B.R. No. 32105 was one of ten Class E2 tank engines designed by L. B. Billinton and built by the London, Brighton and South Coast Railway from 1913 to 1916 to supersede the older Class E1 engines (**Plate 268**). They were originally condensing and had Weir feed pumps. The first five engines had short side tanks of 1,090 gallon capacity but long tanks carrying 1,256 gallons were fitted to the second five, as shown here.

246. L.N.E. No. 68472 was one of forty built 1900–01 for the North British Railway and their Class D (L.N.E. Class J.83). M. Holmes was their designer. They were used for shunting and transfer freight duties and were always (noisily) in evidence at the larger Scottish passenger stations such as Glasgow (Queen Street) and Edinburgh (Waverley). They were the largest and most powerful North British 0—6—0T and most had vacuum and Westinghouse brakes.

247. L.M.S. No. 16348 was one of one hundred and forty-nine standard shunting tank engines of the Caledonian Railway. J. Lambie designed them but they were first built by McIntosh in 1895 and the first nine had condensing apparatus for the Glasgow Underground. This was removed in 1920 by Pickersgill who built the last twenty engines of the Class in 1916–22.

248. L.M.S. No. 7210, with Belpaire boiler and condensing apparatus. This was one of sixty Midland Railway tank engines built between 1899 and 1902 to the designs of S. W. Johnson. As built they had round-top boilers, Salter safety valves on the dome and two-thirds of the Class was built with condensing apparatus for working in the London area. From 1919 onwards, all received Belpaire boilers and later, pop safety valves but the pressure, 160 p.s.i. remained the same.

249. L.M.S. Between 1924 and 1931 more than four hundred Belpaire 0—6—0 Tank engines, known as "Jinties" were built under Henry Fowler's direction for the London Midland and Scottish group. They were basically the same as the Midland engines (above) but had larger saddle-supported smokeboxes, 1,200 gallon side tanks and 2¼ ton bunkers. They were used for shunting and at one time worked the North London passenger services. A number were allocated to Bromsgrove for banking on the Lickey Incline, and B.R. Nos. 47303 and 47301 are shown on this duty.

250. L.N.E. No. 586, Class J50. There were one hundred and two engines in this Class designed by H. N. Gresley. Twenty were rebuilds of Class J51 built for the Great Northern Railway, 1913–22, with 18in diameter cylinders, 4ft 2in diameter boilers and 3 ton bunkers. One of these original engines was superheated. J50's had 4ft 5in boilers and the bunkers carried 4¾ tons of coal. They were built in batches with detail differences between 1926 and 1937, and were known as the "Ardsley Tanks".

0—6—0ST 2F 3F 4F

251. L.M.S. B.R. No. 51404. One of the most successful and simple rebuildings ever, produced the excellent Lancashire and Yorkshire Class 23 saddle tanks. Between 1891 and 1900, J. A. F. Aspinall rebuilt two hundred and thirty of Barton Wright's 0—6—0 tender engines of 1876–78. A backward extension of the frames carried a bunker of nearly 2 tons capacity and the saddle tank capacity was 970 gallons.

252. L.N.E. B.R. Departmental Locomotive No. 2 (ex 68816). In 1897, H. A. Ivatt introduced Class J13 of the Great Northern Railway, a saddle tank design with domed boiler and during the next fifteen years, eighty-eight were built, ultimately becoming L.N.E. Class J52/2. Forty-nine older Stirling domeless saddle tanks were also rebuilt after 1922, to become L.N.E. Class J52/1 and some of these had condensing apparatus.

253. L.N.E. B.R. No. 68062 and 68049. The Hunslet Engine Company designed for the Ministry of Supply these powerful and useful engines and, between 1943 and 1946, several hundreds were built by private builders. In 1946 the London and North Eastern Railway purchased seventy-five of them and classified them J94. The saddle tank carried 1,200 gallons of water and the bunker $2\frac{1}{4}$ tons of coal.

254. Great Western. B.R. No. 4673 was representative of eight hundred and sixty-three pannier tank engines of the 5700 Class built between 1929 and 1950 to the designs of C. B. Collett. They were the successors to a long line of similar, if smaller, engines which were scrapped as they became time-expired. Like all the pannier tanks, they had Belpaire boilers but not all had top feed and engines built before 1933 had the smaller standard cabs. Water capacity was 1,200 gallons, the bunkers held $3\frac{1}{4}$ tons of coal and the maximum axle load was $16\frac{3}{4}$ tons. Nos. 9700–9710 had condensing apparatus (**Plate 257**).

255. Great Western. B.R. No. 6403 on an auto train leaving King's Sutton. The Great Western developed many services worked by auto (push-and-pull) trains. As the older engines for these services wore out, they were replaced by modern 0—4—2 tanks (**Plate 214**) and by 0—6—0 pannier tanks built between 1930 and 1932. The latter were of two classes: the 5400 Class, twenty-five engines with 5ft 2in wheels, and the 6400 Class, forty engines with 4ft $7\frac{1}{2}$in wheels, both designed by C. B. Collett. Coal and water capacity was the same in each class, $3\frac{3}{4}$ tons and 1,100 gallons.

256. Great Western. B.R. No. 8461 working a coal train in South Wales. F. W. Hawksworth's 9400 Class was the last of the Great Western pannier tank family. Ten were built at Swindon in 1947 and these engines were superheated. During the next nine years, a further two hundred, without superheaters, were built by outside contractors. They had short pannier tanks holding 1,300 gallons of water and the bunker capacity was $3\frac{1}{2}$ tons. Maximum axle load was $19\frac{1}{4}$ tons compared with $16\frac{3}{4}$ tons of the 5700 Class. They were the tank engine version of the Collett 2251 Class (**Plate 41**).

257. Great Western. In 1932, one of the 5700 Class engines was fitted with smaller pannier tanks, Weir feed pump and condensing apparatus for working over the Metropolitan lines. Next year Swindon built ten new engines, Nos. 9701—9710, for these duties but the reduction in length of the tanks was compensated by designing for them a side and pannier tank having a water capacity of 1,230 gallons. **Plate 257** shows No. 9705. The rebuilt engine received similar tanks and became No. 9700.

258. L.M.S. Several years after the 1923 Amalgamation this Caledonian engine still carried its original number, 531. It was one of J. F. McIntosh's dock shunters of which two only were built in 1911 as Class 498, but Pickersgill built a further twenty-one in 1918. With a wheelbase of only 10ft and a tractive effort of 18,000 lb, they were ideal and powerful engines for work in the dock areas.

259. L.M.S. No. 11272 was one of ten dock shunting engines built to Henry Fowler's designs in 1928 for the London Midland and Scottish Railway. A standard Midland G5 Belpaire boiler was fitted. The tractive effort was 18,400 lb and the wheelbase only 9ft 6in. The trailing axle had Cartazzi radial axle boxes and the coupling rods were ball jointed allowing 165ft radius curves to be negotiated.

260. L.N.E. No. 5089. Great Central Railway Class 5A, L.N.E. Class J63. Seven shunting tanks were built between 1906 and 1914 to J. G. Robinson's designs, mainly for service in the docks at Immingham. The wheelbase was 12ft and the first two engines had condensing apparatus, for what reason is not now ascertainable. This was later removed.

261. L.N.E. No. 8328 North British Railway Class F, L.N.E. Class J88. There were thirty-five of these dock shunters built from 1905 to 1919 to the designs of W. P. Reid. They had wood block buffers in order to prevent buffer locking on sharp curves, and their wheelbase was 11ft. The later engines had minor modifications and the pop safety valves replaced the old "lock up" valves of the North British. A few had Drummond boilers with the safety valves on the dome.

262. L.M.S. No. 11546. In 1897, J. A. F. Aspinall's outside cylinder shunting engines were built at Horwich by the Lancashire and Yorkshire Railway. They had Allan Link Motion inside the frames, single slide bars, the wheelbase was 12ft and they were among the first British locomotives to have Belpaire boilers. From 1917 onwards all twenty engines in the class were rebuilt with double slide bars and round-top boilers of the same type as those on the 0—6—0ST (**Plate 251**).

263, 264 and 265. Great Western.

Outside cylinder 0—6—0 tank engines built by the Great Western Railway were confined to the three classes shown on this page. The 1361 Class, **Plate 264 (centre)**, consisted of five 0—6—0 saddle tanks with round-top boilers and having a wheelbase of 11ft. They were built in 1910 under the direction of G. J. Churchward and were a modernised version of nine similar engines (1392 Class) taken over by the Great Western from the Cornwall Minerals Railway in 1877. These old engines became time-expired in 1934 and their replacements were five new pannier tank engines with Belpaire boilers, the 1366 Class, **Plate 263 (top)**. They were built to the designs of C. B. Collett and had inside Stephenson Link Motion and vacuum pumps worked off the right hand crosshead. The wheelbase was 11ft and the long pannier tanks carried 830 gallons of water.

The last of the Great Western outside cylinder tank engines were nine built after nationalisation to the designs of F. W. Hawksworth in 1949, the 1500 Class. Although a standard No. 10 saturated taper boiler was incorporated, the design was quite different from previous G.W. practice. Two outside cylinders had 8in diameter piston valves driven by outside Walschaerts valve gear, the axle load was 19 tons 14 cwt, and the wheelbase 12ft 10in. Economy in construction and use of materials was evident in the welding of many parts and the absence of running plates. The side tanks carried 1,350 gallons of water and the bunker 3¼ tons of coal. **Plate 265 (bottom)** shows No. 1505 with empty stock at Paddington where most of the class were employed as station pilots.

266. L.M.S. B.R. Nos. 58860 and 58856 working an enthusiasts' special train on the Cromford and High Peak Line. In 1879, the first of thirty outside cylinder 0—6—0T was built at Bow Works to the designs of J. C. Park for freight duties on the North London Railway. The wheelbase was 11ft 4in and the tank capacity 956 gallons. They were strongly built and in 1931, when they belonged to the London Midland and Scottish Railway, two of them were sent to work on the steep gradients of the Cromford and High Peak Line. Others followed and they worked on the line well into the Last Days of Steam.

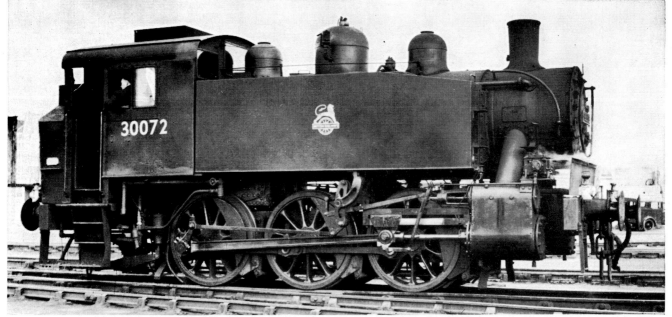

267. Southern. B.R. No. 30072. During the Second War, three American builders, H. K. Porter, Davenport and Vulcan supplied five hundred and fourteen bar-framed 0—6—0T to the U.S. Transportation Corps. These useful and sturdy engines worked in many theatres of war and after the end of hostilities most of them were taken over by European countries where many are still at work. In Britain, the Southern Railway purchased fourteen of them in 1946, and after modifications to cabs, bunkers and brakes they were sent to work in Southampton Docks, replacing the old 0—4—0T (**Plate 213**). The engines were saturated and the wheelbase was only 10ft.

268. Southern. No. 2129, London, Brighton and South Coast Class E1. Seventy-nine were built 1874–91 to W. Stroudley's designs, and re-boilered by D. E. Marsh. Tank capacity was 900 gallons, bunker capacity 1½ tons. For service in the West Country, in 1927 ten were built with lengthened frames, larger cabs, bunkers and tanks and with a Class N pony truck, surplus from Woolwich (**Plate 83**) under the bunker. Tank capacity was now 1,260 gallons and bunkers carried 2¼ tons of coal. **Plate 269 (below)** B.R. No. 32695 Class E1R assisting a Class N up the 1 in 37 gradient from Exeter (St. David's) to Exeter (Central).

270. Southern. B.R. No. 30757 EARL OF MOUNT EDGCUMBE, was one of two 0—6—2T built in 1907 by Messrs. Hawthorn Leslie for the Plymouth, Devonport and South Western Junction Railway. In 1927, the Southern intended to buy more engines of this design for service in the West Country, but the rebuilding of the Brighton Class E1 described above, proved a better and cheaper course and provided locomotives with a maximum axle load of only 14¼ tons.

271, 272 and 273.
Southern. The London, Brighton and South Coast Railway owned one hundred and thirty-four 0—6—2 side tanks with radial wheels. The first design was due to W. Stroudley but one engine only appeared in 1891 and during R. J. Billinton's term of office as C.M.E. sixteen more engines of this Class E3 with 4ft 6in coupled wheels were built in 1894—5, these being Billinton's own design. Although intended for freight duties, they were as frequently used in passenger service and the next engines of the type had 5ft diameter coupled wheels. These were R. J. Billinton's Class E4 of which seventy-five were built between 1897 and 1903. **Plate 271 (top)** shows B.R. No. 32566 of this class with Marsh boiler and extended smokebox, with which all the class was ultimately rebuilt. 1902—4 saw the production of thirty 0—6—2T with 5ft 6in wheels especially for heavy passenger traffic, and these were Class E5. Class E6 appeared in 1904 and twelve were built. **Plate 272 (middle)** shows B.R. No. 32415 of this class which was identical with Class E5 but had coupled wheels of 4ft 6in diameter and was intended for freight duties. All of Billinton's radial tanks originally had flat smokeboxes as seen in **Plate 272**. D. E. Marsh rebuilt a few engines of each of Classes E4, E5 and E6 with much larger boilers and extended smokeboxes. Thus, four Class E4 were rebuilt to E4X with 170 p.s.i. boilers of the Class I2 4—4—2T; four Class E5 received boilers of Class C3 0—6—0 freight engines and became E5X; two Class E6 also received C3 boilers becoming E6X and **Plate 273 (lower)** shows Southern No. 2411 of this class. The appearance of the other reboilered "X" classes was similar.

274. L.N.E. No. 1711 North Eastern Railway Class U, L.N.E. Class N10. Twenty of these engines of Wilson Worsdell's design, went into traffic in 1902–03. They were the tank engine version of his Class P1 (L.N.E. Class J25) and like that class had boilers standard with Class C (L.N.E. Class J21) but none of the tank engines was superheated. The North Eastern had two other classes of 0—6—2T which were tank engine versions of Class C and many of which were built as 2-cylinder compounds.

275. L.N.E. No. 9526 North British Railway Class A, L.N.E. Class N15/1. In 1909, W. P. Reid introduced six 0—6—2T with $4\frac{1}{2}$ ton bunkers for banking duties on Cowlairs Incline. These were L.N.E. Class N14 and they had safety valves on the dome. A further six engines were built in 1910 but with safety valves over the firebox and larger cabs, and these became L.N.E. Class N15/2. Between 1910 and 1920 another sixty-three engines were built with smaller coal bunkers of $3\frac{1}{2}$ tons capacity for general freight duties and these were classed N15/1. Thirty more were built 1923–4 by the L.N.E.R.

277. L.M.S. B.R. No. 58892 working a push-and-pull train in South Wales. This was one of F. W. Webb's Coal Tanks of which three hundred were built by the London and North Western Railway between 1881 and 1890. They had Stephenson Link Motion and slide valves between the cylinders. Although the coupled wheels were only 4ft 3in diameter these stout little engines were widely used on local passenger duties especially in L.M.S. days.

278. Great Western. B.R. No. 56. The 0—6—2 Side Tank was the principal main line motive power of the railways of South Wales and some of the best examples were those designed by Hurry Riches for the Rhymney Railway. Although coupled wheels were seldom more than 4ft 6in diameter, the 0—6—2 tanks did much passenger work and did it very competently. After the 1923 Amalgamation the Great Western provided most of the South Wales 0—6—2 tanks with Belpaire superheater taper boilers and No. 56 is a typical example of such rebuilding.

276 (lower, opposite). Great Western. B.R. No. 5667 working a coal train in South Wales. Conceding the preference of the South Wales railways for the 0—6—2T for both freight and passenger duties, C. B. Collett put into service two hundred 5600 Class locomotives during the years 1924 to 1928. They had Belpaire superheater taper boilers, 8in diameter piston valves, and the coupled wheels were 4ft 7½in diameter.

279. L.M.S. B.R. No. 41983 on an up freight train on the Tilbury Line. Thomas Whitelegg designed the 0—6—2 tank engines for the London Tilbury and Southend Railway. Six were built by the North British Locomotive Company in 1903, another four in 1908 and Beyer Peacock delivered the last four in 1912 after the railway had been taken over by the Midland. The first ten engines were originally named.

280 and 281. L.N.E. The Great Eastern suburban tank engines of Class L77 (L.N.E. Class N7) were introduced by A. J. Hill in 1915 with two engines, one saturated and one superheated. A further ten saturated engines were built in 1921 ; all were later superheated. The L.N.E.R. built more superheated engines until the Class total was one hundred and thirty-four. The seventy-two engines built before 1926 had Belpaire boilers, inside Walschaerts valve gear and short travel valves (N7/1). Next came thirty engines with re-designed Walschaerts gear and long travel valves (N7/2) and finally, in 1927, thirty-two engines with long travel valves and round-top boilers (N7/3). All boiler replacements were with the round-top type. Classes N7/2 and N7/3 had pony trucks instead of radial axle boxes. **Plate 280 (right)** shows No. 2646 (N7/2) at work on the Great Northern line and **Plate 281 (bottom)** No. 2618 Class N7/3.

282. L.N.E. B.R. No. 69434, Great Northern and L.N.E. Class N1, leaving Bradford Exchange with a train for Leeds Central. In 1906, H. A. Ivatt produced his 0—6—2 tank engine No. 190 for King's Cross Suburban services. The weight distribution proved unacceptable for the Metropolitan lines and the next year saw the introduction of ten similar engines in which the side tanks were shortened and the bunker and back tank lengthened. The water and coal capacities remained the same, 1,600 gallons and 4 tons respectively, and the maximum axle load was 18 tons. The boiler was interchangeable with 4—4—0 Class D2 and with 0—6—0's of Class J1 and J5. In all, fifty-six Class N1 were built of which ten were later superheated, retaining their slide valves. All but four had condensing apparatus but this was removed when they were displaced from the London area by more modern engines.

283. L.N.E. B.R. No. 69535, Great Northern and L.N.E. Class N2, on King's Cross outer suburban train. H. N. Gresley's superheated 0—6—2T went into service in 1920 and soon, sixty were at work. The round-top boiler was the same diameter, 4ft 8in, as that of the N1's but was pitched higher to clear the piston valves above the cylinders. A squat chimney and dome were therefore necessary to suit the Metropolitan, Moorgate line, loading gauge, and all were fitted with condensing apparatus. The tank capacity was 2,000 gallons, and the axle load was 19½ tons. Another one hundred and seven engines were built for the L.N.E.R. most with larger chimneys and domes and non-condensing for service in Scotland and on the Great Eastern section. Some had Westinghouse and vacuum brakes. The last ten, built 1929, had short chimneys and domes and were condensing.

284. L.N.E. B.R. No. 69346 Great Central Class 9F, L.N.E. Class N5 on Connah's Quay to Wrexham train at Hope Village. In 1891, T. Parker introduced his Class 9C (L.N.E. Class N5) on the Manchester, Sheffield and Lincolnshire Railway. His previous 0—6—2T Class 9A, L.N.E. Class N4, had Joy's valve gear and round-topped boilers (later rebuilt with Belpaire). Class 9C were built at Gorton with Stephenson Link Motion and were the first British locomotives to have Belpaire boilers. They were not superheated and the pressure was 160 p.s.i. Three engines only were built, but in 1892 the tender engine version appeared, Class 9D, L.N.E. Class J10 (**Plate 31**). From 1894 to 1901 one hundred and twenty-four 0—6—2T were built, mostly by Beyer Peacock & Co. They were identical with Class 9C but were classified 9F by the Great Central Railway which superseded the M. S. & L. on 1st August, 1897. Two were built for the Wrexham Mold and Connah's Quay Railway, later taken over by the Great Central. In 1915 one engine only was superheated and given long side tanks of 2,000 gallons (instead of 1,360 gallons) capacity. Later, a number of engines were superheated and Gresley gave them all "flower pot" tapered chimneys.

285. Great Western. The Alexandra (Newport and South Wales) Docks and Railway Company was amalgamated with the Great Western Railway on 25th March, 1922. The last two locomotives built for the Company were two powerful 2—6—2T, designed and built by Messrs. Hawthorn Leslie in 1920. They were required to haul heavy coal trains but still to be able to negotiate sharp curves and a tractive effort of 23,210 lb was provided with a rigid wheelbase of only 11ft 6in. The engines had saturated Belpaire boilers with 160 p.s.i. pressure and with 20·8 sq ft of grate area. Tank capacity was 1,400 gallons and 3 tons of coal were carried. Engine No. 1205 is shown and this was A.D. No. 36.

286 and 287. Great Western. More than four hundred 2—6—2T of G. J. Churchward's designs were in service on the Great Western Railway. They were of two groups, those with coupled wheels 5ft 3in to 5ft 8in, and those with coupled wheels 4ft 1½in and 4ft 7½in in diameter. The larger engines, 3100 Class, were introduced in 1903 with one saturated engine and eighty-one were built 1905–8. From 1909 they were superheated. They had inside steam pipes, 5ft 8in coupled wheels and the later engines (3150 Class) had larger boilers. The 4300 Class 2—6—0 of 1911 (**Plate 76**) was the tender engine version of the 3150 Class. From 1929, the 4100, 5101 and 6100 Classes were built, all with superheaters and outside steam pipes. In 1938–39 some early engines were replaced, the frames being used in the replacements. **Plate 286** shows B.R. No. 8107, one of ten such engines with 5ft 6in coupled wheels. Five other replacements had 5ft 3in wheels. The work of the big 2—6—2 tanks extended from banking to fast suburban train duties. For steeply graded branch lines the 4400 Class with 4ft 1½in coupled wheels came out in 1904 and in 1906 came the popular 4500 Class with 4ft 7½in wheels, all of which ultimately were superheated. The first seventy-five had 1,000 gallon tanks and the first fifty, inside steam pipes (later given new cylinders and outside steam pipes). There was variation in the size and shape of the bunkers. **Plate 287** shows B.R. No. 4566 as built with outside steam pipes. The last hundred engines had larger tanks carrying 1,300 gallons of water.

288, 289 and 290. L.M.S. After putting into service, in 1927, his successful 2—6—4T Class 4P (**Plate 297**) Henry Fowler, in 1930, introduced one of his worst designs, seventy 2—6—2T of Class 3. With short travel valves and a boiler too small for the work they were called upon to perform—especially the St. Pancras Suburban services—they were regarded as very poor machines. **Plate 288 (top)** shows B.R. No. 40006 in its original form. Tank capacity was 1,500 gallons, coal 3 tons, maximum axle load 16 tons. Some had condensing gear; some later had new cylinders with outside steam pipes.

W. A. Stanier developed the design in 1935 and built one hundred and thirty engines with improved cylinders, long travel valves and taper boilers. Dimensions were mostly the same as for the Fowler engines but the axle load was $\frac{1}{4}$ ton less. These engines were also underboilered and in 1941, four were rebuilt with larger boilers. **Plate 289 (centre)** shows B.R. No. 40142 so rebuilt, leaving St. Pancras for Luton.

A complete change in L.M.S. 2—6—2 tank engine design was made by H. G. Ivatt in 1946. One hundred and thirty engines of a smaller and more compact design were introduced in 1946, the tank engine version of the Class 2, 2—6—0 (**Plate 69**). The wheelbase was shortened and the axle load reduced to $13\frac{1}{4}$ tons. Tank and bunker capacities remained unaltered. **Plate 290 (bottom)** shows B.R. No. 41295 with single-walled taper chimney. The chimneys of Stanier and subsequent L.M.S. engines were double walled, the inside chimney being tapered to suit the blast, the outer chimney parallel for appearance sake. In some of the Ivatt engines the outer wall was dispensed with, leaving only the basic tapered inner chimney. The result was considered ugly and later engines reverted to the double-walled type.

291. B.R. No. 84001 passing Crewe North Junction on a push-and-pull train from Crewe to Northwich. Thirty engines, almost identical with the Ivatt Class 2 (**Plate 290**) were introduced by British Railways. The first ten appeared in 1953 and the last twenty in 1957. The main alteration in the design was in the regulator which was of the two-valve vertical grid type operated by outside rodding. Self-cleaning smokeboxes and hopper ashpans were fitted and some of the engines were equipped for push-and-pull working. As in the case of the L.M.S. engines they were the tank engine counterpart of a Class 2MT 2—6—0 (**Plate 70**).

292. B.R. No. 82022 was one of forty-five 2—6—2T which were built 1952–55 and which were about the equivalent of the Great Western 6100 Class. The boilers were, in fact, almost identical in the two classes, but the maximum axle load of the B.R. engines was only 16 tons 6 cwt compared with $17\frac{1}{2}$ tons of the Great Western engines and the tank capacity was only 1,500 gallons, as against 2,000 gallons. Twenty engines were built in 1954 as tender engines, but were otherwise identical, and these formed the 77000 series, also Class 3MT (**Plate 71**). Most of the 82000 series worked on the Southern region and assisted the Class M7 (**Plate 219**) on empty stock working at Waterloo.

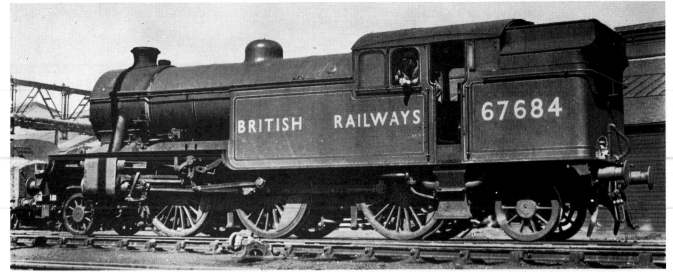

293 and 294. L.N.E. In 1930 H. N. Gresley produced his 3-cylinder 2—6—2 tank locomotive of Class V1. It was similar in power to the 2—6—0's of Class K2. The three cylinders drove the second coupled axle and the 8in diameter piston valves were driven by two sets of Walschaerts valve gear with Gresley's conjugated gear for the inside valve, the drive for this being taken off the forward ends of the outside valves. The tanks carried 2,000 gallons of water, the bunkers 4 tons of coal and the maximum axle load was 19¼ tons. Between 1932 and 1939, ninety-two engines were built, the last ten of which had boilers pressed at 200 p.s.i. instead of 180 p.s.i. as in the other engines. There was no external difference in the two classes. Many of the earlier engines were later fitted with boilers having the higher pressure.

Plate 293 (top). B.R. No. 67684 was one of the engines built with 200 p.s.i. boiler, Class V3.

Plate 294 (bottom). B.R. No. 67680 had the lower pressure boiler and was Class V1. It is here seen fitted with a wire cable to lift the front coupling when banking trains up Cowlairs Incline, Glasgow.

295. Southern. R. E. L. Maunsell's 3-cylinder 2—6—4T Class W, No. 1919, at Ashford Works when new. These fine engines had cylinders and motion interchangeable with those of Classes N1 and U1, and they were the first 2—6—4T on the Southern since the ill-fated Classes K and K1 (page 57). In regular service the fifteen Class W never worked on passenger duties, being used mostly on transfer freight duties in the London area, but some finished up as bankers from Exeter (St. David's) to Exeter (Central). The tanks carried 2,000 gallons of water, the bunkers $3\frac{1}{2}$ tons of coal and the axle load was $19\frac{1}{4}$ tons. They were the last British locomotives to retain bogie brakes. Anti-vacuum valves were removed by Bulleid.

296. L.M.S. B.R. No. 42506 on an up train from Southend. W. A. Stanier's 3-cylinder 2—6—4 tank engines, of which thirty-seven were built, went into traffic on the London, Tilbury and Southend lines in 1934. They had three independent sets of Walschaerts gear and the drive from all three cylinders was to the second coupled axle. The boiler was domeless with the regulator in the superheater header, and on these engines, this arrangement was not altered. The tanks carried 2,000 gallons of water, the bunker $3\frac{1}{2}$ tons of coal, and the axle load was $19\frac{1}{2}$ tons. These engines spent their lives on the L. T. & S. section where they were consistently good performers and they were well-liked by their crews.

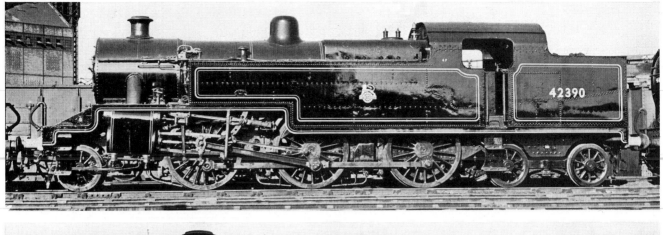

297, 298 and 299. The London, Midland and Scottish Railway had in service six hundred and eight 2-cylinder 2—6—4 tank engines, all of which had 5ft 9in coupled wheels, 200 p.s.i. pressure, 2,000 gallon tank capacity and 3½ ton bunkers. In 1927 Henry Fowler introduced the first of the series with his parallel boiler engines which had long travel valves and adequate bearings and were thus something of an innovation at Derby. They were excellent and popular engines and one hundred and twenty-five were built, the last thirty with side windowed cabs. Some were later given new cylinders with outside steam pipes and **Plate 297 (top)** shows B.R. No. 42390 with this feature.

Plate 298 (centre). L.M.S. No. 2546 was one of W. A. Stanier's taper-boiler 2-cylinder engines of 1935, the first eight of which originally had domeless boilers and low temperature superheaters. Cylinders were slightly larger than those of the Fowler engines but principal dimensions were otherwise identical. The leading wheels formed a Bissel truck. Between 1935 and 1943 two hundred and six were built.

Plate 299 (bottom). B.R. No. 80034. One hundred and fifty-five of these engines were built between 1951 and 1957. They had a shorter wheelbase than either the Fowler or the Stanier engines, approximating that of the Fairburn 2—6—4T (**Plate 300, opposite, top**). The boilers were the same as those of the 4—6—0 Class 4 (**Plate 104**) but with a 9in shorter barrel. They steamed well and never required re-draughting, being able to maintain full boiler pressure at the required rates of working.

300. L.M.S. B.R. No. 42071 on a slow train from Dover to Ashford. C. E. Fairburn, during his short term as C.M.E., modified Stanier's 2—6—4 tank engine design. While keeping the same boiler, cylinders and wheels, the wheelbase was reduced from 16ft 6in to 15ft 4in, enabling curves of 5 chains radius to be negotiated. To keep the same tank and bunker capacities and yet reduce weight, the engine was re-designed. As a result, these engines had an axle load of only 17 tons 2 cwts—12 cwt less than the Stanier and 21 cwt less than the Fowler engines.

301. L.N.E. B.R. No. 67761, Class L1. This was Edward Thompson's 1945 design for a heavy 2-cylinder suburban tank engine, principally for the King's Cross and the Marylebone services. One hundred were built and they had a maximum axle load of 20¼ tons. Tank capacity was 2,650 gallons and the bunker carried 4½ tons of coal; electric lighting was fitted. With a tractive effort of 32,080 lb these were easily the most powerful British 2—6—4 tank engines, but five later had cylinders reduced in diameter by 1¼in. Their coupled wheels were 4in diameter less than the Southern Class W freight tank engines (**Plate 295**).

302. L.N.E. B.R. No. 69808 on a local freight train at Lincoln. J. G. Robinson's Class 9N for the Great Central Railway became Class A5/1 of the L.N.E. They were first built in 1911 for the Marylebone Suburban services and during the next six years, twenty-one were put into service. They had 5ft diameter Belpaire boilers which were standard with those of the rebuilt 4—4—0s of Class 11D (L.N.E. Class D9) and the first engines had Schmidt superheaters, later replaced by Robinson's own superheaters. Ten-inch diameter piston valves above the cylinders were actuated by two sets of Stephenson Link Motion, inside the frames, through rocking shafts. The tanks held 2,280 gallons of water, the bunkers 4¼ tons of coal and the axle load was 18 tons on each coupled axle. Ten further engines were completed in 1923 and these had side-window cabs; the earlier engines later received similar cabs. In 1925–26 a further thirteen engines were built by Messrs. Hawthorn Leslie for the L.N.E.R. for service in the North East. These engines had cut-down chimneys of Gresley design and reduced boiler mountings. They had Westinghouse and vacuum brakes.

303. Southern. B.R. No. 30518 Class H16 was one of five such engines of the London and South Western Railway introduced in 1921 by R. W. Urie for working transfer freight traffic between Feltham hump yard and Brent, Willesden and other London yards. In later years they were to be seen farther afield, even at times, on passenger trains and on Waterloo–Clapham Junction empty stock duties. The cylinders and motion were interchangeable with those of the Class G16 (**Plate 310**) which immediately preceded them and with Urie's Class N15 (**Plate 127**). The axle load was 19¾ tons and the trailing wheels were in a radial truck. Apart from the fitting of Maunsell instead of Eastleigh superheaters these engines were never significantly altered.

304. L.N.E. B.R. No. 69892, 3-cylinder 4—6—2T, Class A8 with Class R (L.N.E. Class D20) boiler.

Vincent Raven designed and put into service on the North Eastern Railway between 1913 and 1921, forty-five 3-cylinder 4—4—4 tank engines of Class D, L.N.E. Class H1. These engines had the drive entirely on the leading coupled axle with three sets of inside Stephenson Link Motion actuating $7\frac{1}{2}$in diameter piston valves. They had power reversers. **304A. (centre)** shows **L.N.E.** No. 1526 in its original form. The Class D ran some important and fastly-timed services, notably between Darlington and Newcastle and the North East Coast and at high speeds, this double bogie design could roll excessively and appeared at times to be unstable. Therefore, from 1931 onwards, H. N. Gresley rebuilt them into 4—6—2T leaving the principal dimensions unaltered. As rebuilt they rode excellently but never appeared to be quite so fast as in their earlier days. Tank capacity was 2,000 gallons, the bunkers carried 4 tons of coal and, as rebuilt, the maximum axle load was $17\frac{3}{4}$ tons.

305. L.N.E. 3-cylinder 4—6—2T No. 1190 North Eastern Railway Class Y (L.N.E. Class A7) with superheater boiler. Vincent Raven's twenty heavy mineral tank engines were his first design for the N.E.R. and they were built at Darlington in 1910. They had what became his usual three cylinder arrangement, in which the drive from all cylinders was to the leading coupled axle and the three piston valves were driven by three sets of Stephenson Link Motion the eccentrics for which were also on that axle. Thus they differed from Worsdell's Class X (**Plate 311**) and they also had 5ft 6in diameter boilers against the 4ft 9in boilers of the 4—8—0T. Most of the Class Y were rebuilt with superheater boilers the pressure then being reduced to 160 p.s.i.

306. L.N.E.R. Between 1902 and 1911, J. G. Robinson put into service eighty-nine 0—8—0 freight engines of Class 8A (L.N.E. Class Q4). They were built without superheaters, but later, many were superheated. The class was largely superseded by Robinson's 2—8—0s, and scrapping began in 1934. In 1942 Edward Thompson rebuilt four of the remaining forty-eight engines into 0—8—0 side tank engines, and in doing so he removed the superheaters. The tank capacity was 1,500 gallons, coal capacity $4\frac{1}{2}$ tons and maximum axle load 19 tons. **Plate 306** shows No. 9927 Class Q1/1. In 1943, a further nine engines were similarly rebuilt but were given larger side tanks carrying 2,000 gallons of water and these were Class Q1/2. **Plate 306A**, page 171, shows one of the superheated 0—8—0 engines from which the tank engines were derived.

307. Southern. B.R. No. 30953 was one of R. E. L. Maunsell's eight Class Z 3-cylinder 0—8—0 shunting locomotives, built at Brighton Works in 1929. They were not superheated and the boiler was one of Brighton's standard types, as used on Classes B2X and C3. Three sets of Walschaerts valve gear were used but the inside valve gear was modified, an extra eccentric being provided to operate the inside radius link. A steam reverser was fitted. Water capacity was 1,500 gallons, coal 3 tons and the axle load c. 17 tons 18 cwt was equal on all four axles. The wheelbase was 17ft 6in but by providing some lateral movement in the leading and trailing axle boxes a curve of $4\frac{1}{2}$ chains could be negotiated. These locomotives were especially useful for hump shunting, but trials with one as a banker from Folkestone Harbour proved the boiler unequal to such sustained demand.

308. Great Western. No. 4286 with inside steam pipes and 4-ton bunker. In 1910, G. J. Churchward introduced the first 4200 Class 2—8—0T for duties in South Wales on heavy, short-distance coal and mineral trains. After prototype trials, twenty engines were built in 1912 and building went on until 1940 when two hundred and five had been put into service. All were superheated and earlier engines had 18½in × 30in cylinders with inside steam pipes. After 1922, cylinders were 19in in diameter with outside steam pipes, older engines receiving them when cylinders were renewed. The coal capacity of the original design was 3 tons; after 1919 extended 4-ton bunkers were fitted to these and to all subsequent engines. Tank capacity was 1,800 gallons and, with 4-ton bunkers, the maximum axle load was 18 tons 14 cwt. Later engines had variations in the shape of the running plates and in the motion bar cross frames.

309. 2—8—2T. No. 7229. In order to widen their sphere of operation, C. B. Collett, in 1934, rebuilt twenty 2—8—0T into 2—8—2T of the 7200 Class. The frames were extended backwards to provide a 6-ton capacity bunker, and increasing the water capacity to 2,500 gallons. Maximum axle load remained unaltered. Fifty-four engines were so rebuilt and varied in details corresponding to the parent engines but all had 19in diameter cylinders and outside steam pipes.

310. Southern. B.R. No. 30492 Class G16, was one of four engines designed by R. W. Urie in 1921 for hump shunting at the Feltham Yard of the London and South Western Railway. The boilers were the same as those of the Class H16 4—6—2T (**Plate 303**) which were built immediately afterwards and cylinders and motion were interchangeable with that class and with the Urie engines of Class N15 (**Plate 127**). Coal, 3½ tons and water capacity 2,000 gallons were the same as for Class H16 but the maximum axle load was less— 18½ tons. These engines spent their whole lives at Feltham and were displaced by diesel-electric shunters.

311. L.N.E. No. 1358 was one of ten 3-cylinder 4—8—0T built in 1909 to the designs of Wilson Worsdell for heavy freight duties on the North Eastern Railway. They were also used for hump shunting at yards in the North East. These engines were North Eastern Class X, L.N.E. Class T1, and a further five engines were built by the L.N.E.R. in 1925. They were all built without superheaters but one received a superheated boiler in 1935. They were of very advanced design for their time, the three cylinders with their steam chests being cast in one piece and steam distribution was by three 8¾in diameter piston valves driven by three sets of Stephenson Link Motion. The drive was divided. Tank capacity was 2,500 gallons and maximum axle load was 17 tons 19 cwt.

312. L.N.E. No. 6173, Class S1/1 superheated, at the top of the "hump". In 1907, J. G. Robinson put into service on the Great Central Railway, four 3-cylinder 0—8—4 tank engines for hump shunting at Wath Concentration Yard. The boilers were interchangeable with those of his Atlantics, and later, his 2—8—0s. The drive was divided, the inside cylinder driving the second axle and the outside cylinders the third; there were three sets of Stephenson Link Motion inside the frames. The water capacity was 3,000 gallons and coal 3 tons; maximum axle load was 18 tons 13 cwt. The four engines, which were Britain's most powerful tank locomotives, were Great Central Class

8H, L.N.E. Class S1/1, and they were built without superheaters. H. N. Gresley later provided them with superheaters and in 1932 fitted No. 6171 with a reversible booster on the trailing bogie, raising the tractive effort from 34,523 lb to 46,896 lb. Bunker capacity was raised to 5 tons but tank capacity reduced by 30 gallons (Class S1/2).

313A. In 1932 two new superheated Class S1/3 engines were put into service each fitted with a booster, which can be clearly seen in this view of No. 2799.

313. The boosters were later removed from all these engines and Nos. 9905 and 9904 (Ex 2799 and 2798) are shown without them.

314. L.M.S. 2—6—0 + 0—6—2 Beyer Garratt locomotive B.R. No. 47994 on an up freight train near Elstree. Three Beyer Garratt locomotives were purchased by the L.M.S. in 1927 to obviate the need for double leading especially on the Toton to Brent coal trains. These engines had fixed coal bunkers, inadequate axle-boxes and bearing surfaces and short travel valves, these features stemming from Derby. In 1930, thirty more engines were delivered and had increased coal capacity from 7 tons to 9 tons, and were, in 1931, supplied with conical bunkers which could be rotated cr oscillated by a 2-cylinder steam engine and a worm drive. These enclosed bunkers were not only self-trimming but also prevented coal dust from blowing into the cab. Unfortunately, no other improvements in design were made and the L.M.S. Garratts were always heavy on coal and maintenance.

315. L.N.E. 3-cylinder 2—8—0 + 0—8—2 Beyer Garratt locomotive No. 69999 at Bromsgrove. In 1925 the largest and most powerful British locomotive made its debut at the Railway Centenary Exhibition. Designed by H. N. Gresley and Messrs. Beyer Peacock it consisted of two 3-cylinder 2—8—0 units identical with Gresley's Class O2 (**Plate 192**) with a 7ft diameter boiler slung in between. This was the first and only 6-cylinder Garratt, the tractive effort was 72,940 lb and the grate area was 56·4 sq ft. This engine was built for banking duties on the 3 miles at 1 in 40 between Wentworth Junction and West Silkstone. When this area was electrified, the Garratt went to Bromsgrove for banking on the Lickey Incline. The large grate proved beyond the capabilities of one fireman and the engine was fitted for burning oil fuel but was soon afterwards withdrawn from service.

242A. L.N.E. North Eastern 0—4—4WT Class B.T.P., L.N.E. Class G6 from which Class 290, L.N.E. Class J77 was rebuilt (**Plate 242,** page 140).

306A. L.N.E. J. G. Robinson's 0—8—0 Class 8A, L.N.E. Class Q4 superheated, from which the 0—8—0T. Class Q was rebuilt (**Plate 306,** page 166). The engine shown was B.R. No. 63217.

316. Southern. Un-rebuilt *Battle of Britain* Class B.R. No. 34064 FIGHTER COMMAND with Giesl ejector. (**Plate 164,** page 105).

TABLE OF DIMENSIONS

Column 1   Plate number in the book

Column 2   Company of origin. This refers to the four pre-nationalisation groups and to British Railways

Column 3   Classification and Power Classification

Column 4   Coupled wheel diameter in inches

Column 5   Cylinder diameter in inches

Column 6   Cylinder stroke in inches. Number of cylinders if over 2 shown thus: (3)

Column 7   Boiler pressure in pounds per square inch. All engines are superheated unless shown in Column 9 thus: N.S. which signifies " no superheater "

Column 8   Tractive effort. This is referred to 85 per cent of the boiler pressure

Column 9   Remarks column. Additional dimensions or details are included in this column

TENDER LOCOMOTIVES

1	2	3	4	5	6	7	8	9
1	B.R.	9F	60	20	28	250	39,670	—
2	L.N.E.	E4/1MT	68	17½	24	160	14,700	N.S.
3	G.W.	3700	80½	18	26	200	17,790	Grate: 20·56 sq ft
4	G.W.	9000/2P	68	18	26	180	18,955	Grate: 17·0 sq ft
5	L.N.E.	D40/1P	73	18	26	165	16,185	Grate: 18·26 sq ft
6	L.N.E.	D11/1.3P2F	81	20	26	180	19,645	Grate: 26·5 sq ft
7	L.N.E.	D11/2.3P2F	81	20	26	180	19,645	Grate: 26·5 sq ft
8	L.N.E.	D16/3.3P1F	84	19	26	180	17,096	Grate: 21·4 sq ft
9	L.N.E.	D20/2P	82	19	26	175	17,025	Grate: 20·0 sq ft
10	L.N.E.	D30/3P	78	20	26	165	18,700	Grate: 21·3 sq ft
11	L.N.E.	D34/3P	72	20	26	165	20,260	Grate: 21·3 sq ft
12	S.R.	T9/3P	79	19	26	175	17,675	Grate: 24·0 sq ft
13	S.R.	D/2P	80	19	26	175	17,450	N.S. Grate: 20·0 sq ft
14	S.R.	E1/3P	78	19	26	180	18,410	Grate: 24·0 sq ft
15	S.R.	D1/3P	80	19	26	180	17,950	Grate: 24·0 sq ft
16	L.M.S.	2P	84½	20½	26	160	17,585	Grate: 21·1 sq ft
17	L.M.S.	2P	81	19	26	180	17,730	Grate: 21·1 sq ft
18	L.M.S.	139/3P	78	20¼	26	180	20,915	Grate: 21·0 sq ft
19	S.R.	L/3P	80	20½	26	160	18,575	Grate: 22·5 sq ft
20	S.R.	L1/3P	80	19½	26	180	18,910	Grate: 22·5 sq ft
21 22	L.M.S.	4P	81	21 L.P. 19 H.P.	26(2) 26(1)	200	22,650	3-cylinder compound. Grate: 28·4 sq ft
23	L.N.E.	D49/4P	80	17	26(3)	180	21,555	Piston valves
24	L.N.E.	D49/2.4P	80	17	26(3)	180	21,555	R.C. valves. Grate: 26·0 sq ft
25 26	S.R.	V/5P	79	16½	26(3)	220	25,135	Grate: 28·3 sq ft
27	S.R.	H2/4P	79½	21	26	200	24,520	Grate: 30·95 sq ft
28	G.W.	2301/2MT	62	17½	24	180	18,140	Grate: 15·45 sq ft
29	L.N.E.	J21/2F	61¼	19	24	160	19,240	Grate: 17·23 sq ft
30	L.N.E.	J15/1P2F	59	17½	24	160	16,940	N.S.
31	L.N.E.	J10/2F	61	18	26	160	18,780	N.S.
32	L.N.E.	J36/2F	60	18¼	26	165	19,690	N.S.
33	L.M.S.	2F	60	18	26	180	21,480	N.S.
34	L.M.S.	25/2F	54	17½	26	140	17,545	N.S.
35	L.M.S.	2F	59	18	26	160	19,420	N.S. R.T.
36	L.M.S.	2F	59	18	26	160	19,420	N.S. Belpaire
37	S.R.	O1/2F	62	18	26	150	17,325	N.S.
38	S.R.	C/2FA	62	18½	26	160	19,520	N.S.
39	S.R.	C2X/2F	60	17½	26	170	19,175	N.S.
40	S.R.	O395/2F	61	17½	26	140	15,535	N.S.
41	G.W.	2251/3MT	62	17½	24	200	20,155	Grate: 17·4 sq ft
42	L.N.E.	J5/3F	62	18	26	175	20,210	N.S.
43	L.N.E.	J6/2P3F	62	19	26	170	21,875	Grate: 19·0 sq ft
44	L.N.E.	J11/2P3F	62	18½	26	180	21,960	Grate: 19·0 sq ft
45	L.N.E.	J11/3.2P3F	62	18½	26	180	21,960	Piston valves

TENDER LOCOMOTIVES

1	2	3	4	5	6	7	8	9
46	L.N.E.	J25/3F	55¼	18½	26	160	21,905	N.S.
47	L.N.E.	J35/3F	60	18¼	26	180	22,080	Slide valves
48	L.M.S.	3F	63	18	26	175	19,890	N.S.
49	L.M.S.	3F	55½	18	26	180	23,225	N.S. Ex F.R.
50	L.M.S.	27/3F	61	18	26	180	21,130	N.S. Grate: 18·75 sq ft
51	L.M.S.	28/3F	61	20½	26	180	27,405	Grate: 18·75 sq ft
52	L.M.S.	812/3F	60	18½	26	180	22,690	N.S. Grate: 20·63 sq ft
53	L.M.S.	294/3F	60	18½	26	180	22,690	Grate: 20·0 sq ft
54	S.R.	700/3F	61	19	26	180	23,540	Grate: 20·36 sq ft
55	L.N.E.	J17/2P4F	59	19	26	180	24,340	Grate: 21·6 sq ft
56 57 58	L.M.S.	4F	63	20	26	175	24,555	Grate: 21·1 sq ft
59 60	S.R.	Q/4F	61	19	26	200	26,160	Grate: 21·9 sq ft
61	L.N.E.	J19/3P5F	59	20	26	170	27,430	Grate: 21·6 sq ft
62	L.N.E.	J20/5F	59	20	28	180	29,045	Grate: 26·5 sq ft
63	L.N.E.	J26/5F	55¼	18½	26	180	24,640	N.S. Grate: 20·0 sq ft
64	L.N.E.	J27/5F	55¼	18½	26	180	24,640	Grate: 20·0 sq ft
65	L.N.E.	J39/4P5F	62	20	26	180	25,665	Grate: 26·0 sq ft
66	L.N.E.	J38/6F	56	20	26	180	28,415	Grate: 26·0 sq ft
67	L.N.E.	J37/5F	60	19½	26	180	25,210	Grate: 19·8 sq ft
68	S.R.	Q1/5F	61	19	26	230	30,080	Grate: 27·0 sq ft
69	L.M.S.	2	60	16½	24	200	18,515	Grate: 17·5 sq ft
70	B.R.	2	60	16½	24	200	18,515	Grate: 17·5 sq ft
71	B.R.	3	63	17	26	200	21,490	Grate: 20·3 sq ft
72	L.N.E.	K2/4MT	68	20	26	180	23,400	Grate: 24·5 sq ft
73	B.R.	4	63	17½	26	225	24,170	Grate: 23·0 sq ft
74 75	L.M.S.	4	63	17½	26	225	24,170	Grate: 23·0 sq ft
76 77	G.W.	4300/4MT	68	18½	30	200	25,670	Grate: 20·56 sq ft
78	S.R.	K/4P5FB	66	21	26	180	26,580	Grate: 24·8 sq ft
79 80	S.R.	N/4P5F	66	19	28	200	26,035	Grate: 25·0 sq ft
81 82	S.R.	U/4P3F	72	19	28	200	23,865	
83	S.R.	U1/4P3F	72	16	28(3)	200	25,385	
84	S.R.	N1/4P5F	66	16	28(3)	200	27,695	
85 86	L.M.S.	6P5F (5MT)	66	21	26	180	26,580	Grate: 27·5 sq ft
87	L.M.S.	6P5F (5MT)	66	18	28	225	26,290	Grate: 27·8 sq ft
88 89	L.N.E.	K3/4P6F	68	18½	26(3)	180	30,030	Grate: 28·0 sq ft
90	L.N.E.	K4/5P6F	62	18½	26(3)	200	36,600	Grate: 27·5 sq. ft
91	L.N.E.	K5/5P6F	68	20	26	225	29,250	
92	L.N.E.	K1/1.5P6F	62	20	26	225	32,080	Grate: 27·9 sq ft

TENDER LOCOMOTIVES

1	2	3	4	5	6	7	8	9
93	L.N.E.	K1/5P6F	62	20	26	225	32,080	
94 95 96 97	L.N.E.	V2/7P6F	74	18½	26(3)	220	33,730	Grate: 41·25 sq ft
98 99	L.N.E.	V4/4MT	68	15	26(3)	250	27,420	Grate: 28·5 sq ft
100	L.N.E.	B12/3.4P3F	78	20	28	180	21,970	Grate: 31·0 sq ft
101	L.N.E.	B17/1.4MT	80	17½	26(3)	180	22,485	Grate: 27·5 sq ft
102	L.N.E.	B2/5P4F	80	20	26	225	24,865	Grate: 27·9 sq ft
103	S.R.	N15X/4P	81	21	28	180	23,325	Grate: 26·68 sq ft
104 105	B.R.	4	68	18	28	225	25,100	Grate: 26·7 sq ft
106	G.W.	4000/5P	80½	15	26(4)	225	27,800	Grate: 27·0 sq ft
107 108 109	G.W.	4900/5MT 6959/5MT	72	18½	30	225	27,275	Grate: 27·0 sq ft
110	G.W.	6800/5MT	68	18½	30	225	28,875	Grate: 27·0 sq ft
111	G.W.	7800/5MT	68	18	30	225	27,340	Grate: 22·1 sq ft
112 113	L.N.E.	B1/5MT	62	20	26	225	26,880	Grate: 27·9 sq ft
114 115	L.N.E.	B16/1.5MT B16/2.5MT	68	18½	26(3)	180	30,030	Grate: 27 sq ft
116 117 118 119 120 121	L.M.S.	5	72	18½	28	225	25,455	Grate: 27·8 sq ft (116) Grate: 28·6 sq ft (117–121)
122	S.R.	H15/4P5F	72	21	28	180	26,240	Urie. Grate: 30 sq ft
123	S.R.	H15/4P5F	72	21	28	180	26,240	Maunsell. Grate: 28 sq ft
124	S.R.	S15/6F	67	21	28	180	28,200	Urie. Grate: 30 sq ft
125	S.R.	S15/6F	67	20½	28	200	29,855	Maunsell. Grate: 28·0 sq ft
126	S.R.	N15/5P	79	20½	28	200	25,320	Drummond Rebuilt Maunsell. Grate: 30 sq ft
127	S.R.	N15/5P	79	22	28	180	26,245	Urie. Grate: 30 sq ft
128	S.R.	N15/5P	79	20½	28	200	25,320	Maunsell. Grate: 30·0 sq ft.
129 130 131	B.R.	5	74	19	28	225	26,120	Grate: 28·7 sq ft
132 133	G.W.	1000/6MT	75	18½	30	280	32,580	Grate: 28·84 sq ft
134	L.M.S.	6P5F	81	18	26(3)	200	26,520	Grate: 30·5 sq ft
135 136	L.M.S.	7P	81	17	26(3)	250	29,570	Grate: 31·25 sq ft
137 138	L.M.S.	7P	81	18	26(3)	250	33,150	Grate: 31·25 sq ft Grate: 31·25 sq ft
139	L.M.S.	6P5F	81	17	26(3)	225	26,610	Grate: 29·5 sq ft
140 141	L.M.S.	6P5F	81	17	26(3)	225	26,610	Grate: 31·0 sq ft

TENDER LOCOMOTIVES

1	2	3	4	5	6	7	8	9
142	L.M.S.	7P	81	17	26(3)	250	29,590	Grate: 31·25 sq ft
143	S.R.	LN/7P	79	16½	26(4)	220	33,510	Grate: 33·0 sq ft
144	S.R.	LN/7P	75	16½	26(4)	220	35,300	
145 146	G.W.	4073/7P	80½	16	26(4)	225	31,625	Grate: 30·28 sq ft
147 148	G.W.	6000/8P	78	16¼	28(4)	250	40,285	Grate: 34·3 sq ft
149	L.N.E.	A1/1.8P6F	80	19	26(3)	250	37,400	Grate: 41·25 sq ft
150 151	L.N.E.	A3/7P6F	80	19	26(3)	220	32,910	Grate: 41·25 sq ft
152 153 154	L.N.E.	A4/8P6F	80	18½	26(3)	250	35,455 33,616	Grate: 41·25 sq ft Inside cylinder 17in diameter
155	L.N.E.	A2/1.7P6F	74	19	26(3)	225	36,385	Grate: 41·25 sq ft
156	L.N.E.	A2/2.8P7F	74	20	26(3)	225	40,320	Grate: 50·0 sq ft
157	L.N.E.	A2/3.8P7F	74	19	26(3)	250	40,430	Grate: 50.0 sq ft
158 159	L.N.E.	A2/8P7F	74	19	26(3)	250	40,430	Grate: 50·0 sq ft
160 161	L.N.E.	A1/8P6F	80	19	26(3)	250	37,400	Grate: 50·0 sq ft
162	S.R.	MN/8P	74	18	24(3)	250	33,495	B.P. orig. 280
163	S.R.	MN/8P	74	18	24(3)	250	33,495	Grate: 48·5 sq ft
164	S.R.	BB/7P5F	74	16⅜	24(3)	250	27,715	B.P. orig. 280
165	S.R.	WC/7P5F	74	16⅜	24(3)	250	27,715	Grate: 38·25 sq ft
166 167	B.R.	7P6F	74	20	28	250	32,150	Grate: 42·0 sq ft
168 169	B.R.	6P5F	74	19½	28	225	27,520	Grate: 36·0 sq ft
170 171	B.R.	8P	74	18	28(3)	250	39,080	Grate: 48·6 sq ft
172 173	L.M.S.	8P	78	16¼	28(4)	250	40,285	Grate: 45·0 sq ft
174 175 176	L.M.S.	8P	81	16½	28(4)	250	40,000	Grate: 50·0 sq ft
177	L.M.S.	8P	81	16½	28(4)	250	40,000	Ivatt. Grate: 50·0 sq ft
178	L.N.E.	Q6/6F	55½	20	26	180	28,800	Grate: 23·0 sq ft
179	L.N.E.	Q7/8F	55¼	18½	26(3)	180	36,965	Grate: 27·0 sq ft
180	L.M.S.	G2/7F	53½	20½	24	175	28,045	Grate: 23·6 sq ft
181	L.M.S.	7F	56½	19½	26	200	29,745	Grate: 23·6 sq ft
182 183	G.W.	2800/8F	55½	18½	30	225	35,380	Grate: 27·22 sq ft
184	G.W.	4700/7F	68	19	30	225	30,460	Grate: 30·28 sq ft
185	L.M.S.	7F	56½	21	28	190	35,295	S. & D. J.
186	L.N.E.	O4/1.7F	56	21	26	180	31,325	Grate: 26·24 sq ft
187	L.N.E.	O1/8F	56	20	26	225	35,520	Grate: 27·9 sq ft
188 189 190	L.N.E. L.N.E. L.N.E.	O4/5.7F O4/7.7F O4/8.7F	56	21	26	180	31,325	

TENDER LOCOMOTIVES

1	2	3	4	5	6	7	8	9
191	G.W.	R.O.D./7F	56	21	26	185	32,200	Grate: 26·24 sq ft
192	L.N.E.	O2/3.8F	56	$18\frac{1}{2}$	26(3)	180	36,740	Grate: 27·5 sq ft
193	L.M.S.	8F	$56\frac{1}{2}$	$18\frac{1}{2}$	28	225	32,440	Grate: 28·6 sq ft
194	B.R.	WD/8F	$56\frac{1}{2}$	19	28	225	34,215	Grate: 28·6 sq ft
195	L.M.S.	Unclassified	$55\frac{1}{2}$	$16\frac{3}{4}$	28(4)	180	43,315	Lickey banker
196	B.R.	WD/8F	$56\frac{1}{2}$	19	28	225	34,215	Grate: 40·0 sq ft
197 198 199	B.R.	9F	60	20	28	250	39,670	Grate: 40·2 sq ft
200 201 202	L.N.E.	W1/8P7F	80	20	26(3)	250	41,435	Cylinders 19in diameter after 1955. Grate: 50·0 sq ft

TANK LOCOMOTIVES

1	2	3	4	5	6	7	8	9
203	L.N.E.	Y4/0F	46	17	20	180	19,225	N.S.
204	G.W.	3F	$45\frac{1}{2}$	16	24	170	19,510	N.S.
205	L.M.S	0F	$45\frac{3}{4}$	15	22	160	14,635	N.S.
206	L.M.S.	21/0F	$36\frac{3}{8}$	13	18	160	11,335	N.S.
207	L.N.E.	Y9/0F	44	14	20	130	9,845	N.S.
208	L.M.S.	0F	44	14	20	160	12,115	N.S.
209	G.W.	0F	41	14	22	160	14,305	N.S.
210	G.W.	0F	43	15	21	150	14,010	N.S.
211	L.M.S.	0F	46	$15\frac{1}{2}$	30	160	14,205	N.S.
212	S.R.	C14/0P	36	14	14	150	9,720	N.S.
213	S.R.	B4/1F	$45\frac{3}{4}$	16	22	140	14,650	N.S.
214	G.W.	1400/1P	62	16	24	165	13,900	N.S.
215	L.M.S.	1F	$53\frac{1}{2}$	17	24	150	16,530	N.S.
216	L.N.E.	Z5/0F	48	14	20	160	11,105	N.S.
217	S.R.	O298/0P	67	$16\frac{1}{2}$	20	160	11,050	N.S.
218	S.R.	O2/0P	58	$17\frac{1}{2}$	24	160	17,235	N.S.
219	S.R.	M7/2P	67	$18\frac{1}{2}$	26	175	19,755	N.S.
220	L.M.S.	W/1P	54	14	20	150	9,255	N.S.
221	L.M.S.	1P	64	18	24	140	14,460	N.S.
222	L.M.S.	2P	67	18	26	160	17,100	N.S.
223	L.M.S.	2P	69	18	26	180	18,680	N.S.
224	L.N.E.	G5/1MT	$61\frac{1}{4}$	18	24	160	17,265	N.S.
225	S.R.	H/1P	66	18	26	160	17,360	N.S.
226	L.M.S.	2P	68	18	26	180	18,955	N.S.
227	L.M.S.	2P	68	18	26	180	18,955	N.S.
228	L.N.E.	F6/1MT	64	$17\frac{1}{2}$	24	180	17,570	N.S.
229	L.N.E.	F5/1MT	64	$17\frac{1}{2}$	24	180	17,570	N.S.
230	S.R.	O415/1P	67	$17\frac{1}{2}$	24	160	14,920	N.S.
231	L.M.S.	79/3P	78	19	26	170	17,390	N.S.
232	L.N.E.	C12/1MT	68	18	26	175	18,425	N.S.
233	L.N.E.	C15/2P	69	18	26	175	18,160	N.S.
234	L.N.E.	C16/2P	69	19	26	165	19,080	

TANK LOCOMOTIVES

1	2	3	4	5	6	7	8	9
235	L.N.E.	C13/2P1F	67	18	26	160	17,100	
236	L.N.E.	C14/2P1F	67	18	26	160	17,100	
237	S.R.	G6/2F	58	17½	24	160	17,235	N.S.
238	S.R.	A1X/0P	48	12	20	150	7,650	N.S.
239	S.R.	P/Unclassified	45⅛	12	18	160	7,810	N.S.
240	L.N.E.	J69/1.2F	48	16½	22	180	19,090	N.S.
241	L.N.E.	J72/2F	49¼	17	24	140	16,760	N.S.
242	L.N.E.	J77/2F	49¼	17	22	160	17,560	N.S.
243	L.M.S.	1F	55	17	24	150	16,080	N.S.
244	S.R.	R1/2F	61	18	26	160	18,780	N.S.
245	S.R.	E2/3F	54	17½	26	170	21,305	N.S.
246	L.N.E.	J83/2F	54	17	26	150	17,745	N.S.
247	L.M.S.	782/3F	54	18	26	160	21,215	N.S.
248	L.M.S.	3F	55	18	26	160	20,835	N.S.
249	L.M.S.	3F	55	18	26	160	20,835	N.S.
250	L.N.E.	J50/4F	56	18½	26	175	23,635	N.S.
251	L.M.S.	23/2F	54	17½	26	140	17,545	N.S.
252	L.N.E.	J52/2.3F	54	18	26	170	21,735	N.S.
253	L.N.E.	J94/4F	51	18	26	170	23,870	N.S.
254	G.W.	5700/3F	55½	17½	24	200	22,515	N.S.
255	G.W.	6400/2P	55½	16½	24	180	18,010	N.S.
256	G.W.	9400/4F	55½	17½	24	200	22,515	
257	G.W.	9700/3F	55½	17½	24	200	22,515	N.S.
258	L.M.S.	498/2F	48	17	22	160	18,015	N.S.
259	L.M.S.	2F	47	17	22	160	18,400	N.S.
260	L.N.E.	J63/Unclassified	42	13	20	150	10,260	N.S.
261	L.N.E.	J88/0F	45	15	22	130	12,155	N.S.
262	L.M.S.	24/1F	48	17	24	140	15,285	N.S.
263	G.W.	1361/0F	44	16	20	150	14,835	N.S.
264	G.W.	1366/1F	44	16	20	165	16,320	N.S.
265	G.W.	1500/4F	55½	17½	24	200	22,515	N.S.
266	L.M.S.	2F	52	17	24	160	18,140	N.S.
267	S.R.	USA/3F	54	16½	24	210	21,600	N.S.
268	S.R.	E1/2F	54	17	24	170	18,560	N.S.
269	S.R.	E1/R.1P2F	54	17	24	170	18,560	N.S.
270	S.R.	757/1P2F	48	16	24	170	18,495	N.S.
271	S.R.	E4/2MT	60	17½	26	170	19,175	N.S.
272	S.R.	E6/3F	54	18	26	175	23,205	N.S.
273	S.R.	E6X/3F	54	18	26	170	22,540	N.S.
274	L.N.E.	N10/3F	55¼	18½	26	160	21,905	N.S.
275	L.N.E.	N15/1.3MT	54	18	26	175	23,205	N.S.
276	G.W.	5600/5MT	55½	18	26	200	25 800	
277	L.M.S.	2F	51	17	24	150	16.530	N.S.
278	G.W.	4F	54	18½	26	200	28,015	
279	L.M.S.	69/3F	63	18	26	170	19,320	N.S.

TANK LOCOMOTIVES

1	2	3	4	5	6	7	8	9
280	L.N.E.	N7/2.3MT	58	18	24	180	20,515	
281	L.N.E.	N7/3.3MT	58	18	24	180	20,515	
282	L.N.E.	N1/2MT	68	18	26	175	18,430	N.S.
283	L.N.E.	N2/3P2F	68	19	26	170	19,945	
284	L.N.E.	N5/2MT	61	18	26	160	18,780	N.S.
285	G.W.	4MT	55	19	26	160	23,210	N.S.
286	G.W.	8100/4MT	66	18	30	225	28,165	
287	G.W.	4400/3MT	49½	17	24	180	21,440	
288	L.M.S.	3MT	63	17½	26	200	21,485	
289	L.M.S.	3MT	63	17½	26	200	21,485	
290	L.M.S.	2MT	60	16½	24	200	18,515	
291	B.R.	2	60	16½	24	200	18,515	
292	B.R.	3	63	17½	26	200	21,490	
293	L.N.E.	V3/4MT	68	16	26(3)	200	24,960	
294	L.N.E.	V1/3MT	68	16	26(3)	180	22,465	
295	S.R.	W/6F	66	16½	28(3)	200	29,450	
296	L.M.S.	4MT	69	16	26(3)	200	24,600	
297	L.M.S.	4MT	69	19	26	200	23,125	
298	L.M.S.	4MT	69	19⅝	26	200	24,670	
299	B.R.	4	68	18	28	225	25,515	
300	L.M.S.	4MT	69	19⅝	26	200	24,670	
301	L.N.E.	L1/4MT	62	20	26	225	32,080	1954: B.P. 200 in some, Cylinders 18¾ in some others
302	L.N.E.	A5/1.3MT	67	20	26	180	23,750	
303	S.R.	H16/6F	67	21	28	180	28,200	
304	L.N.E.	A8/3MT	69	16½	26(3)	175	22,940	
305	L.N.E.	A7/3F	55¼	16½	26(3)	160	26,140	
306	L.N.E.	Q1/1.5F	56	19	26	180	25,645	N.S.
307	S.R.	Z/6F	56	16	28(3)	180	29,375	N.S.
308	G.W.	4200/7F	55½	18½	30	200	31,450	
309	G.W.	7200/8F	55½	19	30	200	33,170	
310	S.R.	G16/8F	61	22	28	180	33,990	
311	L.N.E.	T1/5F	55¼	18	26(3)	175	34,080	N.S.
312	L.N.E.	S1/1.6F	56	18	26(3)	180	34,525	
313	L.N.E.	S1/3.6F	56	18	26(3)	180	34,525	
314	L.M.S.	Garratt	63	18½	26(4)	190	45,620	
315	L.N.E.	Garratt UI	56	18½	26(6)	180	72,940	

LOCOMOTIVE CLASSIFICATION

Steam locomotive classification can be broadly divided into three parts:

(1) an indication of the type, number of axles and any special structural features, (descriptive classification).

(2) an indication of the power of the engine, based mainly on the nominal tractive effort (T.E.) but often including, in freight locomotives, some indication of brake power. This is usually referred to as the load classification.

(3) an indication of the static axle load or of the dynamic augment in terms of route classification or route availability (R.A.).

The pre-grouping Companies varied greatly in their approach to the problems of classification. Most had some form of load classification, often disregarded in practice. Some companies descriptively classified groups of engines taking cyphers and figures from the works order numbers while others, such as the Lancashire and Yorkshire, gave an indication of type by class numbers, or as the North Eastern, by single letters followed by numerals indicative of a major design change in a type, e.g., the 4—6—0s of classes S, S1, S2, S3.

On the GREAT WESTERN RAILWAY, locomotives were usually referred to by their group names *Halls*, *Manors*, *Castles*, *Kings*, etc., and where engines were not named, the reference was to the engine number of the first of class, e.g., " forty-three hundred ", " sixty-one hundred tank " or sometimes as " 43xx ", " 61xx ".

On route availability and power classification, the system was more exact. For the first of these, the system was divided up into five route categories according to the maximum axle load which could be accepted. These categories were indicated on the cab sides of all locomotives by coloured discs, except for the lowest grade with an axle loading of under 14 tons which was not indicated. Otherwise:

A Yellow disc indicated an axle loading 14 to 16 tons.

A Blue disc indicated an axle loading up to 17 tons 12 cwt.

A Red disc indicated an axle loading over 17 tons 12 cwt.

A Double Red disc indicated an axle loading of 22 tons 10 cwt and was applicable only to the *King* Class.

Superimposed on the coloured disc was a capital letter indicating the power classification of the locomotive in " power units ". A power unit was the product of multiplying the nominal tractive effort (85 per cent boiler pressure) in tons by the diameter of the driving wheels in feet. In practice, it worked out *nearly* as follows:

Power unit A was applied to engines with T.E. up to 18,500 lb.
    ,,   ,, B ,, ,, ,, ,, ,, ,, ,, ,, 20,500 lb.
    ,,   ,, C ,, ,, ,, ,, ,, ,, ,, ,, 25,000 lb.
    ,,   ,, D ,, ,, ,, ,, ,, ,, ,, ,, 33,000 lb.
    ,,   ,, E ,, ,, ,, ,, ,, ,, ,, ,, 38,000 lb.
Special   ,, ,, ,, ,, ,, ,, over 38,000 lb.

Engines with T.E. below 16,500 had no power unit.

After grouping, the four companies adopted different systems of classifying their locomotives. The Great Western went on with the system described above.

The SOUTHERN RAILWAY had a confused system of letters and numbers which relied for identification mainly on the fact that generally the engines of the three principal constituent companies kept to their original areas. Thus there were two entirely different types bearing the classification E1, one a rebuilt 4—4—0, the other an 0—6—0 tank engine. On the Eastern Division confusion was worse as there were, for example, 0—6—0T and 0—4—4T each of Class R1, and referred to as the South Eastern R1 and the Chatham R1. On the other hand, several classes consisted of locomotives which did not even have all the same basic dimensions and differed considerably in many other ways. Examples were Class N15 which was composed of six groups of engines and Class H15 in which there were five groups, all with major differences between them.

On the South Western Division there was, in addition, a " Haulage Classification " according to tractive effort, " A " being applied to the most powerful engines and " J " the least powerful. Tank engines were grouped as " K " except for the two Feltham classes (G16 and H16) which were " A ". The system was generally ignored. When locomotives were transferred from one division to another, loading was based on tractive effort and braking power when working unfitted freight trains. A comparison was then made with existing classes already at work in that division.

When new locomotives were being designed, discussion took place regarding the loadings and the required acceleration for the duties to be undertaken. This was translated by the Chief Mechanical and Electrical Engineer into terms of wheel diameter, number and size of cylinders, boiler pressure and so on. The resulting locomotives were then practically investigated by Locomotive Inspectors who carried out coal consumption and load tests.

On the Southern Railway it was always the Locomotive Running Department who made the decisions as to what classes should be used to power particular trains, and there was no reference to this on engine diagrams except where specific loading tables were laid down for freight trains, mainly for braking power. No maximum load was laid down for passenger locomotives.

The LONDON AND NORTH EASTERN RAILWAY had by far the most comprehensive descriptive classification of any of the four companies. A capital letter indicated the wheel arrangement from A = 4—6—2 to Z = 0—4—2T. Numerals followed the letter in such a way that the types of each constituent company were grouped together in descending order of coupled wheel diameter. For example, B1 was a Great Central 4—6—0 with 6ft 9in coupled wheels, B6 had 5ft 8in wheels and B9 had 5ft 3in wheels. Next came B12 to B16 which were ex North Eastern 4—6—0's in the same order. Many of the classes were divided into Parts signified by an oblique after the class number. Thus S1/1 was Robinson's 3-cylinder 0—8—4 tank engine and S1/2 was the same but fitted with a booster. The division of classes into parts, however, was by no means consistent and depended a lot on local requirement. A different tender, different types of springs, different chimney height were made into Parts but in other cases considerable differences were ignored and no division into Parts was made. As an example of this, Class D40 consisted of non-superheater 4—4—0's of 1899 and also of superheated engines built in 1920.

Power or load classification on the L.N.E.R. was originally different for the three areas. A tractive effort/braking classification was evolved for the Southern Area in which freight engines were identified as Class 1 for the lowest powered engines through to Class 8 for the most powerful. A tally was fixed to the front vacuum pipe and this showed the Power Class of the engine. The North Eastern Area had a most complicated system inherited from the old company and which was described in a large manual entitled *Loads of Engines* but no load classification was ever indicated on the engine.

On the L.N.E.R. in Scotland, the North British system of load classification by letters from " A " to " S " shown on cast metal plates affixed to the cab sides was generally used, even after it was superseded officially by a general scheme covering the whole of the L.N.E.R. and based on that of the Southern Area. As on the Southern Railway, the L.N.E.R. load classification applied to freight locomotives only, and except for the high-speed streamlined trains which had restricted loads, no maximum passenger train loads were laid down. However, on certain lines, e.g., the West Highland, as a result of practical tests, definite maximum tonnages were allotted to each class of engine.

In 1947, the L.N.E.R. introduced a system of Route Availability which had been tried out for some years in its Southern Area. This was basically the same as the " coloured disc " classification of the Great Western already described, but it was more detailed. Each locomotive received an R.A. number from 1 to 9 which was directly related to the maximum static axle load, R.A.1 signifying an axle load of not more than $13\frac{3}{4}$ tons, and R.A.9 $21\frac{1}{4}$ tons and over, the intervening numbers showing graduated increases between those two extremes.

The R.A. rating of each locomotive was painted on the cab side, and generally speaking the locomotives of any rating could travel over correspondingly numbered routes or any route with a higher number. So R.A.1 locomotives could travel over any lines in the whole of the system unless specifically forbidden to do so.

On the LONDON, MIDLAND AND SCOTTISH RAILWAY power classification was, in part, derived from that of the Midland railway which was associated with Paget's 1906 Control System. The L.M.S. however, used a curve deduced by the Lancashire and Yorkshire Railway which gave mean effective pressure for various piston speeds and the original L.M.S. classification was based on the *lower* of the two values obtained from

(a) The cylinder tractive effort based on M.E.P. as given on the L. & Y. curve taken at 50 m.p.h. for passenger and 25 m.p.h. for freight locomotives

or

(b) The boiler power based on a maximum combustion rate of 130 lb of coal per square foot of grate per hour, 6·15 lb of steam per pound of coal and steam rates of 25 lb and 20 lb per indicated horsepower for saturated and superheater locomotives respectively.

The Classification Scale was as follows:

Class	*Passenger locomotive* *T.E. in tons at 50 m.p.h.*	Class	*Freight locomotive* *T.E. in tons at 25 m.p.h.*
1P	1·5–2·0	1F	2·85–3·6
2P	2·0–2·5	2F	3·6 –4·35
3P	2·5–3·0	3F	4·35–5·1
4P	3·0–3·5	4F	5·1 –5·85
5P	3·5–4·0	5F	5·85–6·6
		6F	6·6 –7·35

Frictional and vehicle resistances were ignored.

The classification of many L.M.S. locomotives built after 1923 varied from that derived from the above basis, as it was appreciated that with the greatly improved design and performance of modern locomotives a higher classification could be accepted. Such classifications were derived from the known performance of the locomotive concerned.

BRITISH RAILWAYS CLASSIFICATION

When the railways were nationalised in 1948, 20,023 steam locomotives of over 400 different types were taken over and it became immediately necessary to have some form of general power classification. Initially this was instituted on a purely tractive effort basis. For several reasons, especially in passenger and mixed traffic engines, this was not sound practice as it is boiler power rather than calculated cylinder tractive effort which is the determining factor in power output.

The next step, therefore, was the development of the principles of the L.M.S. system which was brought up-to-date in the form of the chart now reproduced on page 184.

This method still resulted in a number of anomalies and in 1949 it was decided to undertake a general re-classification, the practical effect of which was to divide Class 7 locomotives into Classes 7 and 8, to leave Classes 5 and 6 as they were and to spread Classes 4, 3 and 2 over Classes 4, 3, 2 and 1. A few locomotives were completely re-classified, recognition being given to mixed traffic locomotives and anomalies of their previous classification removed.

The basis of this final power classification for British Railways steam locomotives was as follows:

(1) *Passenger and Mixed Traffic Locomotives* were classified according to the value of a FACTOR which was obtained thus:

$$\frac{\text{Free gas area through tube bank} \times \text{Grate area} \times \text{Tractive effort (85\% B.P.)}}{10,000}$$

sq ft   sq ft   lbs

A reduction of 25% in the value of the Factor was made for locomotives with old front-ends and short lap valves.

The value of the Factor depended upon the ability of the boiler to burn fuel in such a way that any unbalance of boiler proportions would penalise the locomotive's power classification in the same way as it would effect its maximum performance.

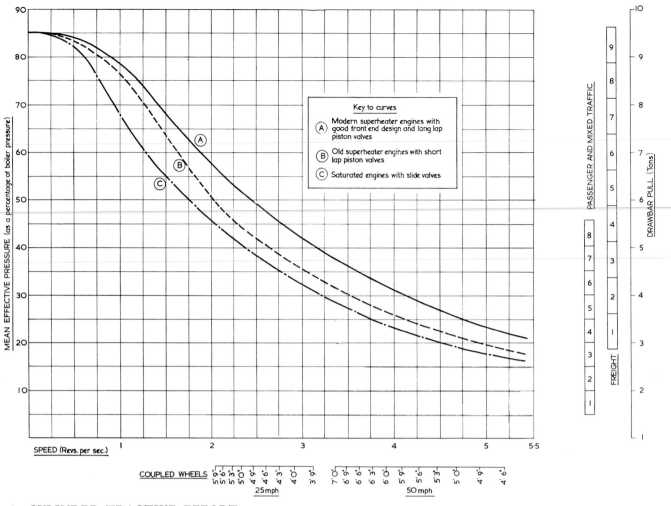

1 CYLINDER TRACTIVE EFFORT

$$\text{CYLINDER TRACTIVE EFFORT} = \frac{Nd^2SP}{4480D} \text{ TONS}$$

WHERE N = Number of cylinders. P = Mean effective pressure in lb per sq in (as given by
d = Cylinder diameter in inches. appropriate curve).
S = Cylinder stroke in inches. D = Coupled wheel diameter in inches.

2 BOILER TRACTIVE EFFORT
ASSUME
  (a) Firing rate of 130 lb per sq ft of grate per hour in narrow fireboxes, and 100 lb per sq ft of grate per hour in wide fireboxes.
  (b) Upper limit of capacity of fireman is 4,480 lb per hour.
  (c) Evaporation under these conditions is 6.15 lb of water per lb of coal.
  (d) Steam consumption per D.B. H.P. hour is 20 lb for superheater engines and 25 lb for saturated engines.
Then the D.B. H.P. developed is given by:—

	Narrow Firebox	Wide Firebox
Superheater engines	40 × grate area	30.7 × grate area
Saturated engines	32 × grate area	24.6 × grate area
Subject to limits imposed by assumption (b).		

The drawbar pull in tons is given by:—
  Passenger and mixed traffic engines .. .. 0.00335 × D.B. H.P.
  Freight engines .. .. 0.0067 × D.B. H.P.

3 POWER CLASSIFICATION
Taking the *lower* of the two drawbar pull figures, obtained as above, the power classification can now be read off the appropriate drawbar pull chart.

As a result of this method, passenger and mixed traffic locomotives were classified thus:

Class	Factor
1	up to 65
2	66–100
3	101–180
4	181–300
5	301–420
6	421–600
7	601–900
8	901 and over

Individual adjustments were made where the known locomotive characteristics were significantly outside any of the above divisions.

(2) *Freight locomotives* were assessed according to whichever was the LOWER of the following VALUES:

(a) Nominal Tractive Effort at 85% Boiler Pressure.

(b) Adhesion Weight divided by 4·5 as representing the maximum drawbar pull which could be sustained at low speeds.

As a result, freight locomotives were classified thus:

Class	Value
1	up to 15,500
2	15,500–19,000
3	19,000–23,000
4	22,500–26,000
5	25,500–28,000
6	27,500–30,000
7	29,500–32,000
8	31,500 and over

This range was extended to Class 9 to provide for the B.R. Standard 2—10—0 locomotives. In a number of cases, the brake power of the locomotive caused an alteration, usually downwards, of the classification. On the Southern Region some locomotives received classifications such as 2FA, or 4FA where their brake power limited their load of loose coupled wagons to less than that of standard Class 2F or 4F locomotives respectively. Similarly Class 4FB indicated that these engines could take more than the usually allocated load over certain routes.

Many locomotives received both passenger and freight power classifications. These, for obvious reasons, were seldom the same, and a so-called Statistical Classification was adopted for reference purposes in which only the main purpose of the locomotive was referred to. For example, the *West Country* Pacifics of the Southern region were Class 7P5F. As their main usage was in express passenger service their Statistical Classification was 7P. Mixed traffic locomotives, however, were usually referred to by their freight classification. The Statistical Classification consisted of six divisions:

Passenger Tender—P	Passenger Tank—PT
Mixed Traffic Tender—MT	Mixed Traffic Tank—MTT
Freight Tender—F	Freight Tank—FT

In some areas these classifications, preceded, of course, by the appropriate power index number, appeared on the cab sides and identical locomotives could often be seen side by side, one designated, for example, " 4 " and another " 4MT ".

It should be emphasised that strict application of the British Railways classification could give rise to anomalies and considerable latitude was given where necessary, to ensure that the classification reflected as accurately as possible the known performance of individual groups of locomotives on the services to which they were allocated.

In addition to the B.R. Classification the regions maintained their former schemes; the Western still had its coloured discs and the Eastern Region engines retained their " letter and number " classes. So, Gresley's streamlined Pacifics will go down in history as Class A4 and it is doubtful if anyone will ever remember them as Class 8P, let alone 8P6F!

LOCOMOTIVE SUPERINTENDENTS AND CHIEF MECHANICAL ENGINEERS OF BRITAIN'S RAILWAYS

LONDON, MIDLAND AND SCOTTISH RAILWAY, AND CONSTITUENT COMPANIES

George Hughes	1923–1925
Sir Henry Fowler	1925–1931
E. H. J. Lemon	1931–1932

Caledonian Railway

Robert Sinclair	1847–1856
Benjamin Connor	1856–1876
George Brittain	1876–1882
D. Drummond	1882–1890
Hugh Smellie	1890
J. Lambie	1890–1895
J. F. McIntosh	1895–1914
W. Pickersgill	1914–1923

Furness Railway

R. Mason	1890–1897
W. F. Pettigrew	1897–1918
D. J. Rutherford	1918–1923

Glasgow and South Western Railway

Patrick Stirling	1853–1866
James Stirling	1866–1878
Hugh Smellie	1878–1890
James Manson	1890–1912
Peter Drummond	1912–1918
R. H. Whitelegg	1918–1923

Highland Railway

William Stroudley	1866–1869
David Jones	1869–1896
Peter Drummond	1896–1911
F. G. Smith	1912–1915
C. Cumming	1915–1923

L. & Y.R.

Sir John Hawkshaw (Consultant)	
Hurst and Jenkins successively to	1868
W. Hurst	1868–1876
W. Barton Wright	1876–1886
J. A. F. Aspinall	1886–1899
H. A. Hoy	1899–1904
G. Hughes	1904–1921

L.N.W.R.

Francis Trevithick and J. E. McConnell, first locomotive Engineers 1846, with Alexander Allan largely responsible for design at Crewe.

Sir William A. Stanier	1932–1944
Charles E. Fairburn	1944–1945
H. G. Ivatt	1945–1947

L.N.W.R. (continued)

John Ramsbottom	1857–1871
Francis William Webb	1871–1903
George Whale	1903–1909
C. J. Bowen-Cooke	1909–1920
H. P. M. Beames	1920–1921
G. Hughes	1922

L.T. & S.R.

Thomas Whitelegg	1880–1910
R. H. Whitelegg	1910–1912

Maryport and Carlisle

Hugh Smellie	1870–1878
J. Campbell	1878–
William Coulthard	*1904
J. B. Adamson	1904–1923

*Date of appointment not known.

Midland Railway

Matthew Kirtley	1844–1873
S. W. Johnson	1873–1903
R. M. Deeley	1903–1909
Henry Fowler	1909–1923

North London Railway

William Adams	1853–1873
J. C. Park	1873–1893
Henry J. Pryce	1893–1908

North Staffordshire Railway

L. Clare	1876–1882
L. Longbottom	1882–1902
J. H. Adams	1902–1915
J. A. Hookham	1915–1923

W. Angus was Locomotive Superintendent at Stoke prior to 1876.

Wirral

Eric G. Barker	1892–1902
T. B. Hunter	1903–1923

LONDON AND NORTH EASTERN RAILWAY, AND CONSTITUENT COMPANIES

Sir Nigel Gresley 1923–1941   E. Thompson 1941–1946
A. H. Peppercorn 1946–1947

Great Central Railway

H. Pollitt	1897–1900
J. C. Robinson	1900–1922

Great Eastern Railway

R. Sinclair	1862–1866
S. W. Johnson	1866–1873
W. Adams	1873–1878
M. Bromley	1878–1881
T. W. Worsdell	1881–1885
J. Holden	1885–1907
S. D. Holden	1908–1912
A. J. Hill	1912–1922

Great Northern Railway

A. Sturrock	1850–1866
P. Stirling	1866–1895
H. A. Ivatt	1896–1911
H. N. Gresley	1911–1922

Great North of Scotland Railway

D. K. Clark	1853–1855
J. F. Ruthven	1855–1857
W. Cowan	1857–1883
J. Manson	1883–1890
J. Johnson	1890–1894
W. Pickersgill	1894–1914
T. E. Heywood	1914–1922

Hull and Barnsley Railway

M. Stirling	1885–1922

Lancashire, Derbyshire and East Coast Railway

R. A. Thom	1902–1907

Manchester, Sheffield and Lincolnshire Railway

Richard Peacock	?–1854
W. C. Craig	1854–1859
Charles Sacré	1859–1886
T. Parker	1886–1893
H. Pollitt	1893–1897

Midland and Great Northern Joint Railway

W. Marriott	1884–1924

North British Railway

†T. Wheatley	1867–1874
D. Drummond	1875–1882
M. Holmes	1882–1903
W. P. Reid	1903–1919
W. Chalmers	1919–1922

North Eastern Railway

E. Fletcher	1854–1883
*A. McDonnell	1883–1884
T. W. Worsdell	1885–1890
W. Worsdell	1890–1910
Sir V. Raven	1910–1922

*Between McDonnell and T. W. Worsdell there was an interval during which the Office was covered by a Locomotive Committee.

†Previous to whom the records are indeterminate.

GREAT WESTERN RAILWAY AND PRINCIPAL CONSTITUENT COMPANIES

Sir Daniel Gooch	1837–1864	William Dean	1877–1902
Joseph Armstrong	{ 1854–1864* { 1864–1877	G. J. Churchward	1902–1921
		Charles B. Collett	1922–1941
George Armstrong	1864–1896*	F. W. Hawksworth	1941–1949

*In charge of standard gauge locomotives of Stafford Road Works, Wolverhampton. The exact dates of George Armstrong's and Dean's terms of service there cannot be definitely ascertained from existing records.

Barry Railway

J. H. Hosgood	1884–1905
H. F. Golding	1905–1909
J. Auld	1909–1922

Rhymney Railway

T. Clements	1858–1863
J. Kendall	1863–1869
J. Canty	1869–1884
R. Jenkins	1884–1906
C. T. Hurry Riches	1906–1922

Brecon and Merthyr Railway

J. T. Simpson	1863–1869
T. Mason	1869–1873
C. Long	1873–1888
E. C. Owen	1888–1922

Taff Vale Railway

From 1840–1873 locomotives were designed and built by private contractors.

T. Hurry Riches	1873–1910
J. Cameron	1910–1922

SOUTHERN RAILWAY AND CONSTITUENT COMPANIES

R. E. L. Maunsell	1923–1937	O. V. Bulleid	1937–1949

London, Brighton and South Coast Railway

—. Statham	?–1845
J. Gray	1845–1847
S. Kirtley	1847
J. C. Craven	1847–1869
W. Stroudley	1870–1889
R. J. Billinton	1890–1904
D. Earle Marsh	1905–1911
L. B. Billinton	1911–1922

London and South Western Railway

J. Woods	1835–1841
J. V. Gooch	1841–1850
J. Beattie	1850–1871
W. J. Beattie	1871–1878
W. Adams	1878–1895
D. Drummond	1895–1912
R. W. Urie	1912–1922

London, Chatham and Dover Railway

W. Cubitt	?–1860
W. Martley	1860–1874
W. Kirtley	1874–1898

South Eastern Railway

B. Cubitt	?–1845
J. Cudworth	1845–1876
A. M. Watkin	1876
R. Mansell	1877–1878
J. Stirling	1878–1898

South Eastern and Chatham Railway

H. S. Wainwright	1899–1913
R. E. L. Maunsell	1913–1922

BRITISH RAILWAYS

Officers holding the rank of Chief Mechanical Engineer or the equivalent title

R. A. Riddles	1948–1953
R. C. Bond	1954–1958
J. F. Harrison	1958–

ACKNOWLEDGEMENTS

Information included in this book has been obtained from very many sources, particularly from conversations over the last forty years with railwaymen of whom the late Hugh le Fleming, the late J. A. Smeddle, the late Sir William Stanier, the late W. H. Stanier, R. C. Bond, Esq., J. F. Harrison, Esq., and C. J. Allen, Esq., have perhaps contributed most.

Answers to many specific questions have been generously supplied by E. S. Cox, Esq., J. R. Hodson, Esq., R. G. Jarvis, Esq., and G. A. Weedon, Esq.

I have repeatedly confirmed my facts from the writings of a large number of authorities who are, alas, far from always in agreement. The *Locomotive Magazine* has been my principal reference book, but I have frequently consulted the excellent and accurate writings of that devoted band of railway enthusiasts of the three major Societies: The Stephenson Locomotive Society, The Railway Correspondence and Travel Society and The Locomotive Club of Great Britain. I have the honour to be a member of all three.

Most of the photographs are from my own collection but I wish to thank the following: British Railways for Plates 1 (frontispiece) and 5, M. W. Early Esq. for Plate 81A, Locomotive Publishing Co. for Plate 83A, L. W. P. Reeves Esq. for Plate 149.

Finally, my thanks are due to a small " committee " of the Locomotive Club of Great Britain who have meticulously read and corrected my typescript.